GOD
of the
GAPS

Finding Faith in the In-between
Spaces of our Journey

Christie Love

NASHVILLE

NEW YORK • LONDON • MELBOURNE • VANCOUVER

God of the Gaps

Finding Faith in the In-between Spaces of our Journey

Published in New York, New York, by Morgan James Publishing. Morgan James is a trademark of Morgan James, LLC. www.MorganJamesPublishing.com

Unless otherwise noted, Scriptures taken from the Holy Bible, New International Version®, NIV®.

Copyright © 1973, 1978, 1984, 2011 by Biblica, Inc.™

Used by permission of Zondervan. All rights reserved worldwide.

www.zondervan.com

The "NIV" and "New International Version" are trademarks registered in the United States Patent and Trademark Office by Biblica, Inc.™

ISBN 9781631952463 paperback
ISBN 9781631952470 eBook
Library of Congress Control Number: 2020939513

Cover Design by:
Christopher Kirk
www.GFSstudio.com

Interior Design by:
Chris Treccani
www.3dogcreative.net

Morgan James is a proud partner of Habitat for Humanity Peninsula and Greater Williamsburg. Partners in building since 2006.

Get involved today! Visit
MorganJamesPublishing.com/giving-back

God of the Gaps

Advance Praise

God of the Gaps pulls the rug from beneath certain Christian platitudes that often plague works about suffering and leaves the reader to wrestle as they try to find God in their "gaps". Although this might sound fearsome, Christie Love makes certain that her readers have the tools to recognize that God is near. Christie does not write from a theological ivory tower; she writes from the depths of her experience. She does not write as someone who "has it all together," yet, her reassuring presence throughout *God of the Gaps* pushes the reader to trust God in their own situation. *God of the Gaps* is a must-read for anyone who is struggling to find the light of God in dark places.

-Ally Henny, The Witness: A Black Christian Collective

I am grateful to Christie Love for sharing her gap lessons with courage, vulnerability, and a good dose of scriptural insight. For all in "the gap" here is help and hope!

-Elisa Morgan, Speaker, Author, Co-Host
Discover the Word and God Hears Her

God of the Gaps is heartfelt and enjoyable to read. If you're in a season of struggle and need encouragement and insight, read this book!

-Wes Taylor, Executive Publisher, Faith Division,
Morgan James Publishing

All of us walk through seasons of the unknown. We wonder if God is with us, if He sees us. And yet it's often in those seasons that God is not only WITH us, but WORKING on us, in our waiting, shaping and molding His kids into their calling and purpose. Christie brings a unique insight to the gaps in our lives, and she gives us a beautiful picture of how God uses those in-between seasons for His Kingdom.

-Kurtis Parks, author of *Sound Check*, Lead Pastor
Bridges Nashville, national recording artist

This book is dedicated to all those who
have struggled, questioned, and wrestled
with faith during seasons of struggle . . .
you are not alone.

Contents

Acknowledgments

This is a project I never wanted to write or share. It started out as journal entries and private blog posts to help me process hard feelings and difficult circumstances. Writing has always been something that brought me peace and clarity. When the world seems chaotic, I can always find comfort at a keyboard. I've dreamed of being a writer and releasing a book since I was a little girl, but this was not the story or the circumstance I ever envisioned would make that dream a reality.

There are so many people to thank for their love and encouragement, not only for this project but also for their constant presence in my life.

To my husband Bob, my greatest cheerleader and supporter. Thank you for always pushing me and refusing to let me give up. I am humbled every day at the privilege to share this journey with you.

To my best friend Holly, my sounding board and huge source of encouragement. I could not have done this without you! Thank you for every coffee and cinnamon roll you brought and every insight you offered. I am blessed to do life with you and your family every day.

To my mom and Jim, who never waivered or left my side in the gap. Thank you for remembering hard days and honoring my hurt. Thank you for every prayer, every hug, and every act of love along the way.

To my sister, my protector and motivator. Thank you for fighting for me when I was too weak to fight myself. Thank you for loving my children like your own and for investing in our struggle in more ways than I could count.

To my grandmother, my prayer warrior. Thank you for your powerful example of faith and prayer. Thank you for always believing in me and supporting me.

To my brother and my father thank you for prayers that spaned the miles, they were felt and received with love. Most of all I want to thank my children—my gap is interwoven with your own. I know our collective gap journey has been less than perfect in so many ways; however, your love and trust on even the hardest of days has motivated me to keep fighting forward.

Andrew, thank you for modeling authenticity and fearlessness for me every day. Thank you for being brave and bold and never staying silent.

Bryson, thank you for your wisdom and insight, your perspective always challenges me to look at the world in a new way. Thank you for the example of courage and hard work to overcome obstacles and follow your dreams.

Katie, thank you for your energy and enthusiasm for life. Thank you for your compassionate heart and willing to use your story to help others around you every day.

Tanah, thank you for the gift of being in your world and for your example of hard work and dedication, which you apply to everything you do in life.

Thank you to so many amazing other amazing family, friends, supporters, Connecting Grounds members and volunteers, and cheerleaders who have breathed life, purpose, and encouragement into me and this project. I am forever grateful for each of you and the role that you have played in my life and my gap journey. Thank you to Cortney Donelson and her gentle touch with editing and cleaning up my heart dump so that it was easier to read and engage with. I am grateful for her encouragement and her perspective.

Thank you to the AMAZING team at Morgan James for believing in the potential of this project and for helping to give it voice. A special thank you to Chris and Jim Howard for your support and faith in me.

The Gap

Gap (n): The space between two objects.
A separation in space.

When you think of the word gap, what is the first image that comes to your mind? For some of us, our minds conjure up familiar images like the gaps between the buildings that shape the skylines of the cities or small towns we call home. Perhaps you think of a person in your life with an endearing gap between their two front teeth that peeks our when they smile at you. Maybe your mind goes to that frustrating gap between your car seat and console, which always seems to attract your phone you drop it and requires acrobatics on your part to retrieve. If you are a sports fan, maybe you think of the perfect gap created for a running back to sneak through during a great play. If you have a favorite show on TV or Netflix, maybe you think of the gap of time you must impatiently endure between one season's finale and the next season's release.

Our lives are full of all kinds of concrete, measurable gaps, which we experience daily. We accept measurable gaps, often with little question, because we see them, or we understand the design or logic behind them.

We can apply this concrete concept to our more abstract life experiences. If a tangible gap is a measurable space between two objects, I would suggest we could also refer to the gaps in our experiences as *the in-between places* in our circumstances. Here are a few examples of what *life gaps* or *in-between places* in our lives can look like:

> *Gaps can be the waiting places between our problems and their solutions.*

> *Gaps can be the searching between our questions and their answers.*

> *Gaps can be the times of struggling between our needs and their provision.*

> *Gaps can be the unmapped journey between our hurt and our healing.*

> *Gaps can be the grief we must endure between sad goodbyes and hopeful hellos.*

Gaps can be the lonely stretches between our hard decisions and the support of others.

Gaps can be the heartaches between our personal desires and God's sovereign designs.

Gaps can be the seasons of wrestling between our plans and God's will.

Gaps can be the seasons of silence between God's promise and His timing.

Gaps can be the waiting between one door closing and another one opening.

As a general rule of thumb, most gaps do not come with warning labels, directional maps, or detailed agendas. When we enter into these seasons of struggle, we have seldom planned or prepared for them. Many times, our gaps feel as though we have been thrust into a complicated maze that often demands big decisions when we feel least qualified or capable to make them. The early days of gaps often feel like we are in a thick fog of emotions that force us to try to feel our way through our unfamiliar new surroundings in an effort to find our physical and emotional bearings. Gaps can make us feel lost, powerless, and overwhelmed.

Most of us want to be in control of our lives and our futures. We want to feel like we are able to dictate the direction we are moving in and the speed at which we are traveling. However, in the gap, we often feel forced to become a back seat driver on a journey to an unknown destination. You are now along for a ride, one often dictated by outside circumstances or other people.

Gaps Are Common Ground

Our self-talk soundtrack during an in-between place is often a constant stream of defensive statements:

I'm a good person.

I do good things.

I don't deserve this struggle.

If you have found yourself thinking these or similar thoughts about your current situation, you are not alone. Our society suffers from *perfection perception*—the false belief that good people should only have good things happen to them. *Perfection perception* wrongly propagates the idea that struggles befall those who deserve them, often those making poor choices or living irresponsibly; conversely, we often believe the misconception that those who make right choices should have problem-free lives.

Perfection perception is a derivative of our modern church culture. Many church services today look more like choreographed performances (with little room to show mistakes or human errors) than authentic worship experiences. Leaders project hip and trendy images, which are so polished and put together that they often appear as if they have stepped out of the pages of a fashion magazine. The social media feeds of popular faith leaders often depict picture-perfect lives that look full of Pinterest decorations and Hallmark happy endings. The struggles, mistakes, failures, and hardships are often hidden offline, away from the watchful eyes of their followers so not to damage personal platforms or church brands. All of this combines to subtly communicate a perception that good things only happen to good people.

Perfection perception has created a virtual checklist of things for us to do to stay in the bounds of blessings—have faith in God, pray daily (especially before meals in public), attend church regularly, give part of your income to the church or other worthy causes, have an active reading plan on your Bible app, and volunteer several times a month in your church and/or community. We have watered down theology and created a false teaching that says, "Following this *Christian Checklist* will insulate a believer from the hurts and pains of the world."

When a person's faith is founded on the misconception that a good God would never let good people enter a gap, they begin to question their faith when struggles come. They begin to wonder if God is punishing them for doing something wrong or if they are wrong about God altogether. These misguided believers enter the gaps of life having to fight dueling battles—the circumstances that brought them into the gap and the validity of their faith and beliefs as they travel through the gap.

Sadly, many who deal with these questions invest more time in trying to find the answers for why they are struggling rather than seeking God as they are struggling.

It's critical to keep this truth in the front of your mind as you find yourself in a Gap.

> Salvation saves us from our sin. It doesn't separate us from this world's struggles.

God sent his own son into the world not to live a safe life but to struggle. While Jesus was on earth, he endured persecution, angry crowds, questions about who he was, and an undeserved death on a cruel cross. Jesus willingly walked the gap between Gethsemane and Golgotha for our benefit. He embraced his struggle because he understood that it was not rooted out of punishment but out of purpose.

Jesus experienced struggle so he was able to share caution with his disciples and all believers with authority. He told them, "Here on earth you will have many trials and sorrows." (John 16:33, NLT)

Jesus did not say ". . .you *may* have many trials and sorrows." No, he said, "you *will*."

We are all imperfect people living in an imperfect world. A world that is sin-saturated and full of brokenness, so despite our Christian Checklists and best efforts to avoid the gaps, each and every person *will* spend some amount of time treading through gaps of some type during their life.

Gaps do not discriminate:

Christian and unbeliever,

Young and old,

Rich and poor,
Healthy and sick.
At one time or another, we will all experience a gap.
In this life, we *will* face problems.
In this life, we *will* experience needs.
In this life, we *will* wrestle with unmet desires.
In this life, we *will* walk through gaps.

Common Gap Entrances

Gaps are common ground. At one time or another we will all become reluctant travelers in a gap. While no two gaps are exactly alike, there are often commonalities in the entrances that our gap journeys originate from:

1. The Health Entrance

Every aspect of your life—your time, your energy, your resources, your abilities, and your social life—can be impacted when you find yourself in a gap as a result of a sudden or chronic health struggle. A part of your body is wearing out or is damaged or diseased and needs to be replaced for you to live the full life you desire, and you are waiting between this need and this new lease on life. You depend on medication, which might be expensive or have life-impacting side effects. You are undergoing treatments to ward off disease and you are wondering how many doses and rounds of side-effects you will have to endure in order for your body to make the arduous journey between health and healing. You wake up every morning to endure another day of chronic and persistent pain, and you are praying for relief. Each day you bravely fight a battle with anxiety or depression, unsure of what will trigger your symptoms and how they will impact your circumstances.

The gap between a diagnosis and a cure can be a frightening and lonely space. Some days feel as though you are moving forward and other days you seem to be moving backward or stuck at a standstill. The gap created by deteriorating health can feel drawn out and full of unexpected twists and turns along the way; those traveling through it often find themselves wrestling with looming opponents like trust, timing, fear, and isolation.

2. The Financial Entrance

When we find ourselves drained of peace and flooded with anxiety and worry because despite our fervent prayers for provision, the bills just continue to snowball without an end in sight, we find ourselves in a gap between our needs and our resources.

We can find ourselves between an expense and the ability to meet that expense. This could be for different reasons. Perhaps the paycheck consistently runs out with days still left in the month. An unexpected job loss undermines our ability to provide for our families. An accident suddenly renders us unable to earn an income. An unplanned expense blindsides our bank account and depletes our savings—the car breaks down, the air conditioner goes out, the roof starts to leak, the scholarship doesn't come through, or a thousand other possibilities that could cause you to face an uncomfortable financial gap.

We can become overwhelmed and grow weary from the heavy burden we are trying to shoulder. Gaps that result from finances can put strain and stress on our health, relationships, priorities, and sense of security. It is easy to lose hope and perspective when we are thrust into a gap through our finances.

3. The Expectations Entrance

We can enter a gap when the reality of our circumstances looks different than the expectations we had for our lives. You could be feeling the pressure to live up to someone else's ideas of who you should be and how you should live your life. You might have relationships that you hoped would be sources of happiness and love; however, their current brokenness and pain are a far-cry from what you had imagined. There might be people in your life with special needs that require a great deal of time and attention from you—children, parents, grandparents, or other loved ones—and this responsibility of taking care of them on a daily basis feels like much more than what you expected. There are many ways your day-to-day reality could look different from the job, home, car, or lifestyle you had always expected, and each of these expectation gaps cause friction within our hearts and minds.

Expectations can be self-imposed or placed on us by others in our lives. No matter how they originate, they are often hard to live with and impossible to meet. Those of us who live under an umbrella of expectation can often find ourselves walking through our gap full of depression and resentment. Often gaps that originate from unmet expectations can lead people to cope with their emotions through unhealthy habits, such as substance abuse, overeating, self-harm, or other dangerous attempts to escape from the expectations we feel unable to meet.

4. The Directional Entrance

Sometimes, we stumble into our gaps, feeling lost and unsure of where to go or what to do next in our lives. We experience a seasonal life change, such as when kids go to school full-time during the days and begin to gain more independence or when they leave home for college. Seasonal changes can begin with the result of losing a job, the need to return to school, or the choice to launch a new career. It can come at the end of a long-term relationship that has defined our life over the years—the unexpected death of a loved one or the sudden separation from someone with whom we have shared life. There are a wide range of circumstances that can push us into a directional gap where we seek wisdom, answers, and a new vision for our lives.

Directional gaps often cause us to feel frustrated and confused. In this place, we are often struggling between our old way of life and a new and uncertain journey opening up before us; we are often tempted to fear the unknown and resist the changes coming our way. While directional gaps are scary, they are also sacred spaces that allow God to move you from where you are now to where He is calling you to go next.

5. The Relational Entrance

You may be walking through a difficult relational gap right now. You could be facing the heartbreak of a marriage that has ended, the foundation on which you built your life has crumbled, and your future plans and dreams are foggy and full of fear. You could be grieving the end of a friendship due to hard circumstances or life changes. You might be dealing with people at work who try your patience and test your grace. Maybe you are facing a parenting gap right now, dealing with the problems of a child who is making poor choices, and you're unsure of how to help get them on the right track. Perhaps you are navigating the gap of grief due to a relationship that was unexpectedly ended or suddenly reshaped by a life-altering accident or loss.

Our lives are full of relationships. When one of them thrusts us into a gap it, can be hard and painful. The hurt and emotions we experience in relational gaps are often intense and difficult to process. Some relationships, damaged by a breach of trust or a hurtful action, can be healed in the gap, while others have to be grieved and laid down before we can move forward.

6. The Dream Entrance

A dream gap is when the distance between your goals and your reality seems insurmountable. You may be overwhelmed by obstacles as you pursue a dream that seems to have come to a dead end. It could be the perfect job you have always pictured yourself doing. It could be buying a house in the ideal neighborhood where you imagined raising your family. It might be the dream of starting your own business or launching an organization to create change in the world. Perhaps you have always dreamed of being married and you find yourself still searching for the right person. Maybe you have always dreamed of being a parent but are walking through the painful gap of infertility, loss, and heartbreak.

The dream gap forces dreamers to wrestle with the hard choices of either giving up or continuing to push forward. It is impossible to know how long we will have to carry a dream or desire before it is able to become a reality, and this unknown makes this particular gap seem long and exhausting. Some dreams are strengthened and clarified in this gap, while others give way to new dreams and direction, born out of the release of their predecessors.

Releasing a dream to God is one of the most painful human experiences we face. It is not easy to let go of something we have hoped for, planned for, and prayed for. At the time, it is hard to imagine how letting go of our dreams can make room for God's divine design for our lives. This gap between our wants and God's will often impacts every area of our life, including our faith and our relationships. Those who travel through a dream gap often find themselves changed through the process of waiting for answers and direction.

Your Gap

There are thousands of storms that impact our world each year and they range in severity from thunderstorms to tornadoes and hailstorms to hurricanes. Storms that have the potential to cause damage to life and property are often given a name. Meteorologists have discovered that people tend to take named storms more seriously and heed their warnings to evacuate or take shelter quicker than an obscure, nameless storm. Naming a storm gives it value, and it stresses the need for us to pay attention.

The same is true in your life.

Your struggle may be hard to face, but it is important to name.

Naming your struggle can help bring obscure emotions into the context of the larger gap you are walking through, so you can see patterns and process through steps, steps that can help you to grow in this place.

What is the name of your struggle?

What is the gap you are navigating right now?

The Trap Of Comparison

Often, we try to minimize our struggle or become indifferent to the gaps we are facing. This temptation to discount our hurt and pain is often the result of feeling that our situation is not *as bad* as someone else's struggle. One of the greatest stumbling blocks in any gap is comparison. It is critical to grasp this truth:

> Gaps are not cookie cutter spaces. Your gap is unique to you and your situation.

There are no bonus points awarded for enduring one type of struggle over another. There are no trophies given for making it through a gap season faster than someone else. You don't get a T-shirt for handling your gap better than another gap traveler. Your gap is your gap; *resist the urge to compare your struggle to someone else's.* Even if two people face the same circumstances at the same time, their journey through the gap will not be identical. How you respond to the gap, process feelings, and react to circumstances is as individual to you as your fingerprint. Every person's struggle is personal and his or her journey to and through gap seasons will look and feel different from another's. This is why gap travelers must understand that *our gaps do not come with score cards and they do not earn grade cards.*

Your worth and your value are not determined by how well you hold it together during a hard season of life. You are not less of a person because you are walking through a gap or facing a struggle. You may have tried to convince yourself that your struggle is not a big deal or not important. If so, please allow me to speak a loving word of challenge to you right now! *Your gap matters.*

Your gap matters to those who love you.

Your gap matters to who you are today and who you will become tomorrow.

Your gap matters to God.

My Gap

If you have picked up this book, then most likely you are facing a struggle of some kind in your life right now. There's a good chance that you are wrestling with fears about your current circumstances. Perhaps your situation is forcing you to question who God is and what is He doing right now. If you are reading this sentence, then chances are you are tired. The kind of tired that you feel in your body, in your mind, and even deep in the corners of your soul.

I get it. I have been there.

I understand, for I am there still.

If you picked this book up by choice or were given a copy from a friend or family member, allow me to say this to you before I say anything else, *I am where you are. I write this book, not as a detached expert but as someone who is also experiencing pain and hardship in life. I, too, struggle with emotions and carry painful scars. I don't write from the top of the mountain, claiming I can guide you to the comforts and pleasure of a happy ending. Rather, this book is written from a place of struggle and heartache.*

If I'm honest, this was not a project I wanted to write. It is a project that I have wrestled with for more than seven years. I fought with it for a bit and then walked away for stretches of time to pray and process how to fully capture the depth and width of the lessons God was teaching me through my personal and painful gap.

Every page of this project was hard as it constantly picked at old scabs and rubs against still healing scars.

Despite numerous prayers to God to be released from this project, He continued to impress on my heart the need to share the powerful perspectives, which He is teaching me through my long gap season. It is for this reason that I'm inviting you to journey with me as we seek God's presence and His purposes in the painful, hard seasons of life.

God of the Gaps is not a biography of my life. Past the next chapter, little will be shared of my personal struggles. Rather, I will unpackage the lessons He has taught me through my struggles, in the hope they help you find some perspective in your own gap.

However, before I can do that, there is some foundational information I feel I need to share with you before we dig in. I want to be honest with you and help you understand where I write from and help you trust the heart behind these words is one that hurts like yours does. If you will allow me, I'd like to share a bit of my story with you in the next chapter. I think it will allow you to see that we have something in common, much to talk about, and a process to learn through the remaining pages.

2

God was...

I know many people assume that because my name appears on the cover of this book that I must have it all together. Trust me, I don't.

The first thing you need to know about me is that I am far from perfect. Like most people, my life has been and continues to be an up and down struggle. I have made more than my share of mistakes and walked through countless messes—many of my own making. I don't pretend to have it all together or have all the answers.

The second critical thing for you to know is that my relationship with God has not been perfect. Though my faith is deep today, it has been forged through the fires of struggle, doubts, searching, and questioning. There were seasons in my life when I rebelled, sinned, and struggled to not only feel God but also follow him. I may be in full-time pastoral ministry today, but trust me, the road to get here was curvy, ugly, bumpy, and full of self-selected detours.

A.W. Tozer once said, "What comes into our minds when we think about God is the most important thing about us." Our thoughts of God create a framework to speak, and that framework shapes our view of God and our view of the world around us. When I pause and think back on just how small and watered down my view of God was for much of my life, my heart hurts.

God Was An Expectation For Me

I like to joke that I was a church member before I was born. My parents rarely missed church services. So when I say *I grew up in church*, I mean from utero. From my first months of life until my teen years, I was there every time there was a service or activity for us to attend. As a young "church kid," I had knowledge of who God was and all the Sunday School stories of what He did in the world.

When I was seven years old, I heard something new while attending Vacation Bible School. It was the first time I can recall hearing about hell. I vividly remember the sudden panic that surged through me when the Southern Baptist pastor passionately talked about how anyone who had not yet received Christ as their personal Lord and Savior could end up in hell—that very day if something were to happen to us on the way home. He explained the only way to avoid such a fate was to come to the front and recite a prayer to invite Jesus into our hearts. I did not just walk, I jogged to the front altars and repeated, out of fear, the words I was prompted to use in order to save myself from an eternity in hell.

No one in my family was surprised by my decision because having faith in God was an inherent expectation in our context. They asked a few simple questions to make sure I understood my choice, and I gave all the right Sunday School answers, which allowed me to be baptized. I had not reached double digits yet, but my eternal future was safe as far as my church and family's views. However, all I knew were facts about the Bible and a palpable fear of hell. I did not fully understand the concept of faith.

God Was Modeled For Me

I watched my parents read their Bible every day. I saw them bow their heads to pray during quiet times or before meals. I sat next to them in the pews on Sunday morning as they dutifully took notes and nodded their heads in agreement with the pastor's teaching.

I was amazed at my grandmother and her ability to recite large sections of scripture from memory and sing almost every hymn on Sunday morning without the aid of a hymnal. She had a deep love for God and respect for the Bible.

I had a front row seat to *people of faith* doing *things of faith* on a regular basis. I looked up to my parents and grandparents, which meant I felt I must mimic the same habits they had. I tried to pray, but no one had really taught me how to talk to God, so I simply brought Him lists of things I wanted or needed Him to do. I tried to read my Bible, but because my grandmother would often talk about how she believed there was only one true translation that should be read, *The King James Version*—she would stress how anyone who read a version other then the King James was a heretic—my first Bible was impossibly hard to understand and I struggled to engage.

Sadly, in an effort to follow their example, my framework for God became cold and cookie cutter. My view of the character of God was a carbon-copy viewpoint of what I heard from and saw modeled in others. It was practical, but it was not personal.

God Was A Calendar Of Events And Social Opportunities

I became the quintessential "church-kid." Our family continued to attend church every Sunday morning, Sunday evening, and Wednesday night. As I grew older, my church activity level increased through participation in the youth group, Handbells, Church Drama, Bible Drill, and the youth choir; however, my personal connection with God did not grow concurrently.

If I am being honest, as a pre-teen, I was not involved in these activities as a way to know God better or worship Him at all. I was at the church every time the doors were open, but it was not because of any connection with God. It because of my connection with my friends. Church was my social sanctuary. It was a place to hang out with friends, develop crushes on cute boys, and have fun together.

God Was A Clearly Defined List Of Rights And Wrongs

Since I was involved in so many activities at church, I began to amass a great deal of head knowledge about the Bible. I memorized all the books of the Bible in order. I could recite the 23rd Psalm from the King James Version. I could sing all four verses of "Victory in Jesus" without a hymnal (just like my grandmother).

I thanked God for my family and my food at every meal. Every night before bed, I repeated a carefully honed list of requests to God that ranged from a puppy to world peace. I listened to Christian music. I did not use bad words. I *tried* to be kind to my younger siblings. I *attempted* to obey my mother and father. I was careful to make sure that I was doing everything that a "church-kid" was expected to do. I guess you could say I was a good rule-follower for the first dozen years of my life.

God Was Too Busy For My Problems

During those first twelve years of my life, things were pretty simple and easy. I grew up in a nice home that reflected our family's middle class status. My midwestern, Bible-belt upbringing kept me protected from much of the painful reality of the world. I didn't really need God's help with anything because there was not really anything that I struggled with up to that point. However, the summer between my sixth and seventh grade year, I had my first encounter with brokenness.

It was at this time that the dreaded word *divorce* entered my vocabulary. Throughout the early years of my life, I thought my parents had a happy marriage; I never saw my parents fight, so I was blindsided by the news, broken during a calm family meeting, that they were no longer in love and my dad was leaving.

Suddenly, I needed God. I needed Him to fix this. I needed Him to end this nightmare for me and restore the comfort and simplicity that was shattered with the prospect of my family breaking apart. I thought that if I prayed hard enough, God would do a miracle in my parent's marriage. I spent weeks and months praying with childlike faith and expectation that God would magically fix my family, because after all, I was a good, "church-kid" who followed all of the rules. I had fallen prey to the *perfection perception*, feeling strongly that I did not deserve the bad things that were happening to me.

God Was Disappointed In Me

It was not only the foundation of my family that was rocked, the weak foundation of my immature faith also took a direct hit. When I needed God the most, He seemed to be too busy or uninterested in answering my prayers and fixing my family. I became angry and bitter toward Him.

Outwardly, I still went to youth camps, mission trips, lock-ins, drama practices, youth group meetings, prayer events at school, and anything else I could find to throw myself into that was church related. I think part of me believed *if I could be good enough,* my dad would want to come back. However on the inside, my "faith" was giving way to doubts, nagging questions, frustrations, and anger.

Outside of our home, I seemed to have it all together. Inside the safety of our home, I often exploded into emotional tirades filled with verbal daggers of anger and hatred toward my family. I was a walking contradiction. Knowing this made me more angry with myself and the person I was becoming. The anger was eating away at my joy and my self-worth. Deep down, I felt God was disappointed in who I was becoming as well.

God Was Distant

Eventually, my internal anger no longer boiled only beneath the surface. It began to pour out into my words and actions on a daily basis and in all areas of my life. My frustrations were no longer contained just at home. I became bolder in my rebellion. I never did anything *really* bad, but I pushed the envelope as far as I was comfortable pushing it. I replaced my youth group friends with new, edgier friends who understood my anger and helped me "express it." I lied to friends and family. I cheated in school. I stole. I cursed. I lowered my standards with boys. I listened to angry music. I snuck out of my house. I hurt the people I loved.

I was an emotional mess. However, I knew deep down the one who I was really angry at was God. He had let me down, and it seemed He did not care about the hurt and the pain I was feeling. He felt far away, and I hated that feeling, which made me more angry at Him.

God Was Manageable

I became a master "wall-builder," never letting people close enough to hurt me. When I sensed they were getting too close or could hurt me by leaving first, I ended the relationship to protect my own heart. This pattern of behavior impacted countless friendships and a handful of dating relationships through the end of high school and the start of college.

However, the relationship I most tried to manage was my walk with God. I would go through periods of wanting to be closer to Him so I saught Him out. I would get involved in youth group, attend faith-based school functions, and listen more intently in church; however, if He started to step on my toes or convict me of my not so godly behaviors, I would push away from Him. I was in a pattern of micromanaging every relationship around me to protect myself from any more heartbreak and hurt.

God Was Waiting To Punish Me

I fell apart while attending a Christian college. I was skipping classes, slacking off in my studies, missing chapel, and letting my relationship with God grow cold. I was tired of being the good, little "church-kid," so for the first time in my life, I explored the party scene and began to embrace a lifestyle I had long avoided. For the first semester and a half of college, I made a long series of one poor choice after another. Those choices resulted in a circumstance that changed everything for me.

I was attending a party at the apartment of an upperclassman. There were lots of cute boys and lots of alcohol that night—a recipe for disaster. As the evening progressed, I found myself in a bedroom, alone with a male athlete twice my size. I know I started the interaction between us with innocent flirting and fun; however, I suddenly found myself unable to stop the speed and direction it was heading. When it was over, I was hurt, humiliated, and embarrassed.

In my unhealthy, depressed mentality, I justified the violence against myself as deserved punishment from God for all the distance and space I put between Him and me. My religious upbringing made it easy to rationalize the word *rape* away and replace it with *repercussion*. From my conservative theological framework, this pain was the repercussion of living a lifestyle I had been taught and raised to avoid.

God Was Going To Bless My Plan A

That party was the catalyst for change in my life. I knew I could not continue down the path I was stubbornly wandering down. I had experienced the pain and consequence of reckless living, and I didn't want to live through anything similar again.

I became serious about school, reinvolved with the church routine, and found a *safe* boy from a good Christian family to date. I developed a plan for my life that could be best summarized, *if I do all the right things, then all the right things will happen to me.* My plan became the pursuit of perfection, and I truly believed God would bless and honor this pursuit.

I decided that the best way to replace a long season of pain over my own broken family was to create a family of my own. I became convinced that the cure to my anger and depression was the All-American dream—marriage, children, house, and job were surely the key to happiness. I was desperate to prove to myself, my family, and my friends that I was capable of a healthy relationship. I needed to know there was something in life that I was not going to fail at, so I got married at the naive age of nineteen to this *safe* boy whom I had known a total of eight months. We quickly started a family, and I quit school to be the *perfect* stay-at-home mom.

I dreamed of rocking happy babies and making delicious dinners at night for my husband who would come home happy from a long day at work. Instead, my reality was days spent pacing the floor with a colicky infant while stressing about how far I could stretch a pound of hamburger for meals that week. I worried constantly about how frustrated my husband would be when he got home over our mounting pile of bills and overwhelming obligations.

God Was Confined To A "Holy Checklist"

Marriage was hard, but I was determined. I wanted God to bless my plan to redeem myself, so I developed a detailed "holy checklist," which I followed religiously as a cheap substitute for a real relationship with God. I prayed daily over the same list of people and petitions. Most days, I carved out time to read my Bible during a quick devotional time. Much like when I was growing up, our young family went to church together every Sunday and Wednesday.

My husband and I were stressed to the max, so we thought the answer was to *serve* to the max. The problem with this kind of shallow service is that it leads us to live lives that are not authentic. We could lead in ministry because our spiritual service convinced people around us that we were healthy and happy. Yes, on the outside, we were serving God. We were in God's house. We were surrounded by godly friends. Privately, our marriage was crumbling under our financial stress, my husband's personal struggles, and my obsession with perfection.

My "holy checklist" routine was not a solution or a source of strength. Even though we went through all the right motions, we failed to do so with the right motives. We were serving God outwardly, but we were failing to make faith in God the foundation of our marriage. As a result, our home became consumed with tension and our marriage was plagued with arguments. I quickly grew frustrated and tired.

Immature and ill-equipped to handle all of the emotions flooding us, I did the one thing I swore I would never do to my children. After seven years of marriage, I made them a statistic of a broken home. I didn't have the strength to keep fighting, so I waved the white flag and gave up. I was disappointed with myself and was sure God must feel the same way about me. I believed I was a failure.

My shame pushed me away from God again. This time I didn't push away out of anger at God but because I figured He was done with me. I believed I'd failed God, and He was angry at my shortcomings and my sin. I avoided His presence because I knew He would shine a light onto the sin and shame I was trying to keep hidden in the darkness of my heart.

A Glimmer Of Hope

Six months into my journey as a single parent, after a long day of trying my best to juggle three young children and an unknown future, I hit rock bottom. I was exhausted. I couldn't sleep at night because my mind was racing through all the possibilities of what could happen, and I raced through my days to try to maintain some amount of control and stability. I was scared. I had more questions than I had answers. My stomach was in knots all the time, eating became a battle. My head pounded daily as the tension in my body matched that of my swirling circumstances. I was feeling overwhelmed with trying to care for three young kids on my own.I did the only thing that I could think to do at the end of a long day. Out of sheer desperation, I cried out to God.

I didn't pray a safe, checklist-style prayer, one where I simply asked God to bless me and threw in a long list of people whom I love. I didn't pray a cold, memorized series of words. For the first time in this "church girl's" life, I prayed a sincere, heartfelt prayer. Leaning against a massive load of unfolded laundry at the top of my stairs, through my sobs, I was honest and humble.

"God, I can't do this on my own. I need you. Please help me."

That simple prayer was the start of the most complex journey of my life. A journey that has led me to a deep awareness of who God really is and how wrong I had been about Him for nearly my entire life. That prayer began my transition from my pre-formatted, checklist-based religion to a *personal, intimate* relationship with God.

Did my circumstances change right away?

No, but my heart began to change.

That simple prayer, which I uttered to God in the hallway of my small townhouse, "God, please help me," unleashed a chain reaction in my life that left no area untouched. That night, as I knelt in the darkness, I felt as though I heard God speak to my heart.

"All you had to do was ask."

All I had to do was ask. I remember letting that statement rebound against the walls that had long been erected in my heart and mind, the ones that kept people at *safe* distances. My life. My plans. My marriage. My pride. My finances. My children. My parenting. My future. My past. My struggles. My relationships. My hurts. My emotions. When was the last time I had asked God for help?

I came to a painful and humbling realization: I had grown up in the church, and I knew the person of God, yet I did not really *know* God *personally.* I had never really experienced His presence because I had never really invited Him to be present. I had been so focused on who I thought that God was that I missed out on experiencing who He really is and how he has been pursuing me all along.

Maybe, like me, you have been so focused on who you have believed God to be that you have not fully seen or experienced who God is. Allow me to introduce you to the God I met and fell in love with during the most difficult gap I have faced in my life.

3

God is . . .

As I have already shared with you, I have struggled in gaps for much of my life; however, it was not until I discovered God IN my gaps that my life was transformed and my relationship with God became deeper and more intimate. You see, my decision to fully surrender to Jesus that night on the floor outside my daughter's bedroom did not mean I had waved a magic wand (nor did Jesus) and my life was made perfect.

In fact, the days, weeks, and months that followed my decision to connect personally to Christ were not easy. It was a long journey of forgiving myself and healing old hurts. In time, renewal did come but not without new gaps to travel through.

God blessed me with a second chance at love and brought a man into my life who was the exact opposite of me in almost every way imaginable. We married, and we each worked hard not to repeat the mistakes I'd made in previous relationships. We struggled to blend two families into one, clumsily stumbling into step-parenting roles. We navigated new relationships, co-parenting, visitation, and transition issues as we tried to make the best of our broken, blended roads. The transition wasn't smooth; both of us made mistakes—lots of them.

Spiritually, I was like a bear awakening from hibernation, ravenous for more than the shallow, superficial sermons and resources I was being offered. My heart craved depth. It seemed the deeper I dove into the love of God and the knowledge of God, the deeper I desired to go. I immersed myself in God's Word with a driving desire to understand Him more and apply His truth to my life. I not only read the Word of God but also wrestled to apply it to my parenting, relationships, and often-challenging circumstances.

God began to use this insatiable hunger to beckon me into full-time ministry. At first, I pushed back from the idea. I felt that I was too broken and too messed up to be used by God in an effective ministry capacity. I tried to give God every excuse I could think of as to why He was calling the wrong person. However, the more I offered excuses the louder He whispered into my heart, *I AM does not call the qualified, I qualify the called.*

In 2011, full of fear, I began a new journey into full-time Christian ministry. As I stepped out of my comfort zone to serve God and use my story of brokenness, our family stumbled into a deep, dark gap—the worst we had faced. This is the painful, hard gap that we are still walking through today as I write these words.

I'm not going to reveal the exact nature of our current gap or what it looks like for our family. To do so is to set us up for the scorecard mentality that we talked about in Chapter 1. Sharing our story might unintentionally cause you to focus more on my circumstances than your own. Sometimes, I do share our story as God prompts me, often in the context of personal conversations. When I do, people tend to respond with disbelief and shock. Many times, I hear, "My struggles seem like nothing compared to yours." That's exactly the sentiment I want to avoid. By withholding the details of our struggle, I'm intentionally leaving space for you to focus on your own gaps without comparison to mine.

This long gap through which I have been journeying has taught me more about the heart of God than any Bible study or sermon ever could. I have learned about the depth of God's love and the tenderness of His care. I have experienced His strength and the peace that can only be found in Him. This gap has changed me completely, inside and out. I am not the same person, wife, mother, or leader that I was when I entered this season. God has used my gap to reshape who I am as I experience more of who He is.

This is what has motivated me to retrace my steps in this painful gap . . . I want to help you see God in your gap. I want more for you than just head knowledge of who God is. I long for you and everyone else who is in a gap to find your own ways to connect with Him and discover Him in this season of struggle and all of the moments to follow. I can promise you this: If you are willing to seek Him in new ways during this gap, your faith, your life, and your journey will never be the same.

Who Is God To You?

I need to ask you some hard questions. I want to encourage you to read each one slowly and pause after reading it to answer honestly in your heart. These are critical baseline questions about where your relationship with God currently stands and only you can answer them. They are not designed to have right and wrong responses but rather to stimulate some honest conversation with yourself and God.

- Do you have a relationship with God today?
- Where does God fit into your gap right now?
- When was the last time you talked to God? What was that conversation like?
- Are you angry with him and blaming him for the gap that you are facing?
- Are you asking hard questions and seeking him for the answers?
- Are you regularly attending church right now?
  - » If so, what is your motivation for going?

» If not, why not?
• Who or what is your greatest source of comfort and strength in your gap? Is it God or is it someone or something else?

I believe there are four kinds of people in the world today:

1. Those who deny God completely.
2. Those who acknowledge His existence but choose not to engage with Him personally.
3. Those who have a personal connection with God that is routine-based and activity driven.
4. Those who have fully surrendered their hearts and lives to God's will and His ways.

> Many times, the category we identify with depends on the gaps we have faced in our lives.

I have talked to countless people over the years who have told me heartbreaking stories of gaps they have traveled through in their lives, stories of abuse, homelessness, loss, grief, pain, and heartbreak. Many of these people have looked at me with sad or suspicious eyes and proclaimed there could be no God because "how could a God allow me to hurt in all the ways I have?"

There are others whom I have sat with who have told me through tears that they grew up in the church and bought into the Sunday School stories of a God who loved them. However, as life got tough and they began to experience gaps, they pushed away from God, angry and bitter at Him for allowing them to hurt.

I have listened to other stories, like mine, from people who said it was in their darkest moment they saw the light of God's glory for the first time. It was not until they hit rock bottom that they looked up and found faith and a personal relationship with Jesus Christ.

> Gaps are often defining seasons and as a response to them, we either push away from God or connect with Him more.

What has your gap done to your relationship with Him?

God Is Constant

Wrap your minds around this concept with me: *No matter what your view of God is, it does not change who God is.*

God's presence is bigger than the small box you try to reduce Him to fit into.

God's sovereignty is not undermined by your persistent doubts.

God's love is not canceled out by your hard questions of Him.

God's grace is not watered down by your anger toward him.

> Bottom line: God is not redefined by your opinion of him; your perspective of God molds and shapes you, not Him.

No matter how angry you are at God, He does not change.

No matter how far you run from God, He does not change.

No matter how much you know about God, He does not change.

No matter how unsure you are about Him, He does not change.

God is constant and consistent.

Theologians call this characteristic of God *immutability,* a term meaning unchangeable. God himself proclaims this aspect of His character in Malachi 3:6 when He states, "For I the Lord do not change..." (NRSV) The writer of the book of Hebrews declares, "Jesus Christ is the same yesterday and today and forever." (NRSV)

Well known 19th Century Baptist Preacher Charles Spurgeon once said of God's unchanging nature, "Consider what you owe to His immutability. Though you have changed a thousand times, He has not changed once."

I am grateful for the comfort we can draw from this truth; nothing we do can alter His love for us. Nothing we face can take away from His glory and His goodness. Nothing we struggle with can subtract from His sovereignty. God is God at all times and in all circumstances. *Our gaps do not change God.*

Of the many names given to God in the Bible, there are several that highlight God's immutability. One of those is *the rock.* The Psalmist uses this term to describe God in Psalm 18:2 saying, "*The Lord is my rock*, my fortress, and my deliverer, my God, *my rock* in whom I take refuge, my shield, and the horn of my salvation, my stronghold."

I live in the fertile land of the middle of America where my perception of rocks was formed by the small rocks I found on the playground or the larger ones lining the shore at the lake. These stones were undoubtedly hard in substance but were a weight and size that could be manipulated. As a result, when I would hear God referred to as *the rock*, I would think of a small stone that can be easily picked up and tossed here or there. Sadly, this image fit with my former view of God—that He existed more for me than I for Him. I could pick Him up when I wanted Him. I could put Him in my pocket for good luck. I could collect Him to take out and look at whenever I wanted to do so. I share this with you because, perhaps like me, your view of God is or has been smaller than it should be. Maybe you have struggled to grasp the value of God's unchanging nature. I don't want you to miss out on it any longer. Seeing God as your constant rock will give you a strong and unshakable foundation upon which to build your faith in God.

David grew up a shepherd boy in the rocky countryside of ancient Israel, a landscape shaped by large boulders and rock formations. David had no doubt sat atop many massive rocks to get a better view of his flock, and he had most likely found shelter from passing storms in the caves and crevices, carved into the landscape by rocks. To

David, rocks were an inherent, unchangeable part of the landscape in which he had grown up, and he was thinking of this as he penned the promise of Psalm 18:2. No doubt many of his childhood memories came from exploring and traversing these massive formations, which were used as hiding places and homes in the ancient world.

Do not miss the tender power of this holy comparison. David knew God to be rock solid, a place of safety and dependability. This view of God Almighty was formed in the gaps of temptation, death threats, sickness, betrayal, and war. David was able to go through each struggle with confidence, knowing God was His unshakable rock. He experienced first-hand that no matter how much the circumstances of his life shifted, God would not and did not change.

It was this understanding of God's unmoving nature that undergirded David's personal relationship with God, a relationship strengthened within the gaps. In fact, the connection David had with God in the gaps was so strong that he earned the nickname *a man after God's own heart.*

God Is Relational

The personal relationship David had with God was not rare. Every single person has an opportunity for that same kind of divine connection. In fact, that is one of the most beautiful aspects of God's consistency—His never-changing desire to have a personal relationship with each man and woman. Pause for just a moment and let that truth wash over you. *The God who created the universe, hung the stars in the sky, molded the mountains with His hands, and carved out the rivers with His fingertips wants to be connected with you personally! He wants to be known by you and desires a connection with you daily.*

It blows my mind each time I dwell on this humbling truth.

Scripture shows us God is relational, both within Himself through the trinity, as well as in His love toward each of us. In the opening words of the Gospel of John, we read of creation, "In the beginning was the Word, and the Word was with God, and the Word was God. He was in the beginning with God." (NRSV) John is referring to Jesus as *the Word* in this passage, making it clear that from the very beginning, there were both eternal father and son, unique in identity and unified in sovereignty. The first two verses of Genesis 1 enlarge this picture to include the Holy Spirit, the third member of the trinity. "In the beginning God created the heavens and the earth. The earth was formless and void, and darkness was over the surface of the deep, and the Spirit of God was moving over the surface of the waters." (NASB)

We refer to God as a triune God, meaning He is three in one. God the Father, Jesus the Son, and the Holy Spirit are equal in their godliness yet diversified in their function. We could spend entire chapters talking about the function and the design of the trinity, but for this discussion, I want to focus on the fact that God himself is inherently relational by divine design. He is in relationship at all times with the members of the trinity and this inherent relational nature is what led Him to create humankind.

God Is Not Going To Force You

Then God said, "Let us make human beings in our image, to be like us." (Genesis 1:26) From the moment mankind was first conceived in the heart and mind of God Almighty, we were created to be like God. When God created man in His image, it was not just a physical resemblance. We were created to have a heart and a mind like God's. Which means that at their creation, both Adam and Eve's minds were focused on the good and the holy because their minds were like God's.

However, one day, the serpent [Satan] came to Eve in the garden God had created, and he began to question her about the singular restriction God had placed on her and Adam. "Did God really say you must not eat the fruit from *any* of the trees in the garden?" Eve responded by clarifying God's command, "We may eat fruit from the trees in the garden, it's only the fruit from the tree in the middle of the garden that we are not allowed to eat." She explained to the serpent that to eat from this restricted tree would mean death for her and Adam.

The serpent quickly retorted, "You won't die!" He then told her that by eating the fruit, their eyes would be opened, and they would become more like God for they would have knowledge of both good and evil at that moment. With Adam there by her side, they bought into this deception and partook from the restricted tree together.

With these bites of disobedience, mankind forever underwent a mental makeover. Mankind was designed for holy fellowship with the God of the Universe. In the garden, before that seemingly innocent bite, there were no distractions or deterrents to that divine design. However, the choice Adam and Eve made ushered sin into the world and undermined the intimacy we once enjoyed with God.

One choice changed everything, but God loved them enough to give them that choice.

He loves each of us enough to let us choose to love Him or reject Him.

The prophet Isaiah penned the words, "Therefore the Lord waits to be gracious to you; therefore he will rise up to show mercy to you. . . " (Isaiah 30:18, NRSV) Stop and ponder that statement: The God of the Universe waits for you.

A.W. Tozer said, "God waits to be wanted." The God who created you will never force himself on you. Rather, out of love, He made a way for us to always come to Him, not just as our God and creator but also as our father and friend.

God Is Our Father

For some of us, thinking of God as our father is hard and confusing because it clashes with the earthly experiences we have had of a father or father-figure. For me, my dad was not around very much during my formative tween and teen years as he built his own career hundreds of miles away. I often struggled with feeling like he didn't care or was too busy for a relationship with me. I brought this perception of a father into my early relationship with God, projecting similar emotions on Him. As I have shared with you already, I often believed God was too busy to be bothered by me.

However, the more I learned about God and His nature, the more I discovered how wrong I was. God does care and He is never too busy for me. Learning to see God and relate to him as my father has been life changing for me.

Through the canvas of Scripture, a tender picture of the father and child relationship that God longs to have with us is clearly painted for us to see. At the end of Deuteronomy as Moses is nearing his death, he implores the nation of Israel to fix their thoughts on God as their father who has protected them and brought them out of Egypt. He writes, ". . .is not he your father, who created you, who made you and established you?" (ESV) David declares in the Psalms, "As a father shows compassion to his children, so the Lord shows compassion to those who fear Him." (ESV) The prophet Isaiah proclaims, "For you are our Father, though Abraham does not know us, and Israel does not acknowledge us; you, O Lord, are our Father, our Redeemer from of old is your name." (ESV)

The Old Testament is full of fatherly pictures of God protecting the Israelites, defending them, guiding them, instructing them, disciplining them, and pursuing them.

In fact, as you read the Old Testament with a mental framework as God the father, you begin to see how the nation of Israel behaves like a teenage child struggling to find his or her way in the world. However, the fatherly relationship between God and humankind takes on a different dimension in the New Testament.

In the Gospels, we read the narratives of Christ's earthly ministry. God the Father sends God the Son into the world not to conquer it but to die for it. Jesus came to earth as God incarnate, God made man. He came to boldly speak truth and to tenderly see and serve the marginalized. He came to show the power of God and make a way for all people to enter into a relationship with God. Iconic paintings like Van Gogh's *Starry Night* or DaVinci's *Mona Lisa* are instantly recognized by those familiar with art as well as those who are not; one could make a case that the Biblical equivalent of these masterpieces is the well-known verse of John 3:16.

"For God so loved the world that he gave his only Son, so that everyone who believes in him may not perish but may have eternal life." (NRSV) We see the reference painted on signs at football games, displayed on decals on the back windows of cars in traffic, and etched on coffee mugs. We see this verse frequently, but when was the last time you really meditated on the powerful statement of love and fatherly sacrifice this verse communicates to us?

In the early 2000s, a retired pastor and well-known author named Eugene H. Peterson published a popular paraphrase of the Bible called *The Message*. It seeks to summarize passages of scripture into more updated language to make the themes of the Bible easier for people to grasp and interact with. It is a beautiful labor of love, making a great compliment to the study of more formal Bible versions. Peterson's rendering of John 3:16 reads, "This is how much God loved the world: He gave His Son, his one and only Son. And this is why: so that no one need be destroyed; by believing in him, anyone can have a whole and lasting life."

God the Father loved you and me enough to send his only son to die for each of our sins. Famed Christian author C.S. Lewis once observed of Jesus' death on the cross, "He died not for men, but for each man. If each man had been the only man made, He would have done no less." Take that statement by Lewis and personalize it. Fill in these spaces with your name and read it aloud, allowing the power of that truth to wash over you for a moment: "Jesus died not for everyone but for me. If I, _____(your name), was the only person in the world, he still would have come and died for me."

With his death on the cross, Jesus simplified the process for us to enter into personal connection with God. No longer, did someone have to keep a long set of rules and rituals. The only requirement to a relationship now is belief. In Romans 10:9–10, the apostle Paul plainly states, ". . .if you confess with your lips that Jesus is Lord and believe in your heart that God raised him from the dead, you will be saved. For one believes with the heart and so is justified, and one confesses with the mouth and so is saved."

At the beginning of this chapter, I asked you if you have a personal relationship with God. If your answer to that question was no, then I want you to fold down the corner of this page right now. If, as you read through the remainder of this book, you begin to see God differently and start to believe the truth that He loves you and wants a relationship with you, I want you to come back to this page and re-read this section.

You can do what Paul is explaining in Romans anywhere and at any time. There are no magic words or sacred locations you must be in to proclaim your faith in Jesus. You can whisper a simple "God, I need you" from an airplane seat, a hospital waiting room chair, the floor of a college dorm room, the front seat of your parked car, or a million other everyday places. God, your Heavenly Father, is ready to meet you any time, anywhere you choose to invite Him in.

Maybe you had a relationship with God at one point but the gaps you have traveled caused you to push away from Him in anger and confusion. Maybe your whisper sounds a little different—more like, "God I am sorry I pushed away, I need you to get through this. I know that you love me and I am coming back to you now."

It could be that your story is more like mine, and you have grown up and spent much of your life in the church; however, this gap you are facing is revealing a shallow connection with the God you are so familiar with.

Perhaps your whisper sounds more like a commitment to go deeper: "God, I have long believed in you but now I long to know you better and more personally. Guide me to a greater understanding of you and intimacy with you."

Keep in mind, God is always there to hear and respond to your prayers; however, He will never push you to say them or come to Him. He will pursue you and find ways to communicate His love to you through music, friends, books, invitations, and countless other means, but He will not force you into a relationship with Him. He loves you so much that He sent his son for you, and He loves you enough to give you the choice to accept Him or reject Him.

This is the most important decision you face in your gap. Will you turn to Him in this season of struggle or will you push away from Him?

Some of the aspects of the gap, which complicate this critical choice, are the strong emotions that overwhelm us and often cloud our perspectives in our gaps. Our feelings can be one of our biggest barriers or greatest blessings in the gap, so let's take some time to explore the divine design of feelings and how they impact our journey and our connection with the God of the Gaps.

4

Permission to Feel

On an unsuspecting Thursday morning in January, I suddenly found myself thrust into the gap between normalcy and never, ever the same. Instantaneously, it felt as though my feet were knocked off solid footing by a tidal wave of emotions. It seemed as though I had been violently grabbed by an invisible, emotional undertow that was so strong, it threatened to drown my soul before I could find my bearings.

A wave of anger hit me and threw off my balance. . .

What just happened!
Was that real?

Right behind it came a wave of frustration. . .

I do not deserve this!
I am a good person!

This isn't fair!
Followed immediately by a strong wave of fear. . .
What am I going to do?
How am I going to live like this?
Then an unexpected wave of sadness. . .
No! This can't be happening to our family!
A wave of worry washed over me. . .
How is this going to be okay?
How am I going to do this?
How will we survive this?

I felt as though I couldn't catch my breath as wave after wave of different emotions slammed into my mind and heart. There were no safe shores to swim toward, no way to save myself from the hurricane of hurt I was facing. In my exhaustion, I gave in and tried to survive by floating on the waves of emotional highs and lows. However, the constant rise and fall of my emotions robbed me of peace, deprived me of sleep, drained my energy, and blocked my perspective.

The more I struggled with this strong tide of emotions, the more tension grew inside me as I simply tried to survive. The greater the intensity of the emotions I had, the less safe I felt to share my feelings with friends, family, or my church. No one knew what to say or how to respond to me so to make others feel more comfortable, I worked hard to hide or minimize my feelings.

The Myth Of The Mask

We live in a culture that has a complicated relationship with emotions. We all experience them; however, many of us feel pressured to downplay our feelings or cover them up all together. After many years of both personal and ministry experience, I believe some Christians feel a unique kind of pressure to cover up their emotions. I would also say that many who do not have a personal relationship with God could trace their disconnect back to an emotional issue they experienced.

I am going to say some tough things out of love in this section. I believe there are some hard truths about modern church culture, which must be spoken for people to find freedom from previous perspectives, ones that have prevented their healing or impeded their connection with God.

First, allow me to frame my critique of these aspects of the church with this important disclosure: I have a deep love for the design of the Church. I strongly believe in the power of the community and fellowship, which the Bride of Christ has to offer a believer to enhance and add value to his or her life. I am deeply passionate about the potential the Church has to radically engage our culture in powerful ways while reflecting the love and mercy of Jesus. I love the Church, and I believe in the Church. However, when I contrast the vision of the Church I read about in the pages of the New Testament with what many modern churches feel like today, there is a deep sense of lament welling up in my spirit. My complicated relationship with the Church began when I was very young.

I can vividly remember driving to church as a child with my parents in the front seat and my two siblings with me in the back, fighting. The three of us would argue all the time—about everything. Yet, we all knew that once we pulled into the parking lot of First Baptist Church, we needed to put on our happy, "church" faces and *pretend* to be getting along.

Looking back, I do not remember a single Sunday School lesson about how to handle my feelings. I clearly recall that certain emotions were always portrayed as bad while others were celebrated. Anger was always framed as a negative or sinful emotion, while joy and happiness were regarded as the evidence of a close relationship with God. Feelings of fear were met with cliché Christian phrases, such as "The Bible says do not fear 365 times, one for each day of the year." While these statements may have been a true piece of Biblical trivia, it also felt dismissive, subtly communicating to a teenager whose house was splintered by divorce that she was not entitled to the fearful feelings she was facing.

The deep emotions of my teenage years sent me into a depressive, rebellious spiral, which my youth group leaders and friends stepped back from instead of into. A dangerous message began to take root in my heart: *My feelings were not welcome at church.*

This message was reinforced in my adult years again and again. I learned to put on my Christian mask of happiness and joy to church or around my church friends. If I acted okay, everything was great. Even in the face of trials and struggles, I would try to *fake it till I felt it.* However, as we traveled further into our gap, I became too tired to maintain false pretenses. I not only allowed people to see the uncensored truth of my fears and depression, I publicly spoke about them. In the church I was attending at the time, my honesty was met with push back and rejection.

I wish my story was unique. Unfortunately, I have had countless conversations with people over the years, which have convinced me that my experience is, sadly, very common. All too often, the Church celebrates happiness, peace, patience, and joy as the expected standard of normalcy, while, raw, difficult emotions and feelings are discouraged, to be tucked out of view and covered up with a manufactured smile and the andectodote of serving frequently and staying busy. While this message may not be vocalized verbatim, it is a dangerous narrative that has been infusing the Church through off-handed remarks, social media comments, and the repetition of Christian catch phrases like these:

If you are feeling depressed, you just need to pray harder.

If you are feeling anxious, your faith must not be strong enough.

Faith and fear cannot coexist.

A good Christian is always full of the joy of the Lord.

If you are depressed, just sit and read your Bible.

The combination of careless comments like these and the inability of many churches and Christians to help people process strong feelings causes many people to feel as though their emotions are unwelcome in a church context or even that they are unwelcome at church altogether.

Church, we can and must do better!

The Church should be the place where we feel most free to be ourselves, drop our pretenses, and be honest about our struggles. We should find commonality with other people at church through our hurts, our experiences, and our feelings, and not in our attempts to protect and cover them up. Within the Church, there should be safety for emotional baggage to be unpacked without fears of backlash or gender stereotyping. Men should feel free to express emotions without being labeled as weak, and women should be able to share feelings without being labeled as overly emotional.

We challenge this perspective by first changing our own understanding of our emotions and the critical role they can and *should* play in our discipleship. Feelings should be a topic talked about in every church to help every believer learn to navigate their emotions rather than feel pressured to cover them up. We should be studying how God gifted humanity with an immense emotional capacity, one God wired into the human mind and heart. Understanding this truth opens deeper connections and conversations with our Creator.

Our Divine Design

You need to know that you have the permission to feel the wide variety of emotions swirling constantly through the gaps in our lives—sadness, anger, frustration, worry, depression, and anxiety. Yes, there will be times when you may feel as if you are drowning in your feelings. There will be moments where the intensity of your emotions can be so strong that they feel suffocating. At times, emotions may overwhelm you and weigh you down. Your emotions may make some days more difficult than others. These days matter just as much to God as the good days.

> Your emotions are God-given, and you don't have to hide them from God or apologize for feeling them or struggling with them.

What are some of the emotions you are wrestling with right now? Have you experienced moments of feeling consumed and overwhelmed by them as you have navigated the in-between places of your gap? I challenge you to fold down the corner of this page, close the book, and simply sit and talk to God for a moment about your feelings. Name your emotions with Him and trust that He cares about each of them.

***

I hope you took a moment to think about some of the emotions you are wrestling with right now. I encourage you to read through these statements and mark the ones that speak truth into your current and specific circumstances:

- God wants us to come to Him with our sadness.
- Your tears are precious to Him and He sees each one.
- God wants us to come to Him amid depression and despair.
- Your struggle is seen and matters.
- God desires for you to talk to Him about your anger.
- Your rage does not push Him away.
- God longs for you to bring Him your deep frustration and hard questions.
- Your toughest question is always welcome, even if the answers aren't easy or don't come.
- God cares about your worries and anxiety.
- Your fears do not disqualify you from a relationship with Him.
- God sees your hurts and your heartbreaks.
- Your difficulties do not offend Him or make Him give up hope for you.
- God watches over your journey to healing.
- You are never alone or abandoned in your gap.

Emotional Magnets

I think of emotions as magnets, each one having the connective power to pull me to the heart of God. At least that is the divine design—that each of our feelings would draw us deeper into a relationship with God. When I feel scared, I connect to Him for assurance. When I feel angry, I connect to Him for perspective. When I am confused, I connect with Him for answers. When I am happy, I connect with Him in praise and celebration. Each emotion I experience can be a conversation, a question, or a moment of worship with God.

It is an amazing thought, especially if you bought into the misconception that God does not care about your feelings or that your emotions had to be hidden or tucked away from God. Not only does God care about your emotions, He was the one who gifted them to you in the first place! The God of the Universe wired you with emotional capacity in hopes that those emotions would add dimension and depth to our connection with Him.

Just as tangible magnets can either connect with something or repel something, our emotions have the same potential. When we are willing to be drawn into the connection with God, our emotions enhance that desire. When we are determined to push away from God in anger, distrust, or lack of faith, then we flip those emotional magnets over, and what was created to connect us is now a catalyst for resistance. In this state, each time you feel upset about your gap you push harder away from God.

The polarity of our emotions is a major factor in our experiences in the gaps of our lives. If we are determined to push away from God during any hardship or struggle we face, then we will go through the gaps full of resentment, determined to solve all our own problems as we wrestle with the wide range of emotions the gap brings. In this place of constant pushing away from God, we often feel exhausted and on edge. For many people who are resisting

God, they seek to escape their overwhelming emotions through substance abuse, sex, cutting, over-eating, or other forms of coping, which attempt to numb or distract them from the feelings they have. These emotionally motivated actions often lead to greater pain and complications in their gaps.

In contrast, when we allow the emotional highs and lows of our gaps to draw us into God, we experience the peace of knowing we have a safe place to take our feelings. We can find rest because we realize our emotions are not burdens for us to bear; rather, they are opportunities to connect with our Creator.

God Waits

I hope you can see how each of your emotions has the potential for a unique connection with God's heart and ability to draw you closer into a relationship with your Heavenly Father. The potential is always there, but God is not going to force Himself on anyone. A.W Tozer once stated, "God waits to be wanted."

While He is aware of your struggle, He waits for you to come to Him. The prophet Isaiah declares this truth, "So the LORD must wait for you to come to him so he can show you his love and compassion." (Isaiah 30:18) God waits to be called on and sought out. He waits to be invited and included in a relationship with you. He does not want you to come to Him simply out of habit or routine. Instead, He craves personal connection with each of us.

Think about your important earthly relationships. Often these are the people who you call to help you sort through big emotions and tough circumstances. Many times, these are the people who you want to celebrate big successes with and seek out their shoulders to cry on when you are struggling. These are people who you trust with your feelings and feel free to be open and honest. God wants that kind of personal connection with you, too. He wants you to come to Him with anything you are facing and anything you are feeling.

In John 15:15, Jesus utters an amazing perspective in red letters, "I no longer call you slaves, because a master doesn't confide in his slaves. Now you are my friends, since I have told you everything the Father told me." Jesus wants to be your friend. What a humbling thought! Wrap your minds around this truth, in the context of that kind of personal, friendship connection, your feelings matter to the God of the Universe and He waits for you to trust Him enough to be honest and real with him about your feelings, your struggles, and your questions.

5

The Tension of Trust

One of the most important ingredients in any healthy relationship is trust. However, trust is often something that must be developed, earned, or cultivated as a friendship deepens over time. This is true for our earthly connections, and it is also true for our relational connection with God. Many believers couple the two terms together and assume that if someone professes faith in God, they must naturally practice trust in Him. While this is a common line of thought, it is important to note that it's not an automatic occurrence. Faith and trust are related to one another yet not interchangeable pieces, but rather, exist as unique building blocks.

Faith and trust differ from one another, yet they also depend on each other. Many times, initial faith is cultivated without trust as someone comes to accept the basic belief that God exists, and as the creator of the universe, He wants a personal relationship with him or her. In this fresh state, faith is often untested and shallow. There is nothing wrong with faith starting out like this; however, faith is not meant to remain shallow and stagnant. Shallow faith is insufficient to support and strengthen us during the gaps of our lives. God desires for us to grow in our knowledge of Him and go deeper in our relationship with him. For this to happen, trust must be added to our relationship with God.

Faith believes that God is real, available, and accessible in this world; trust seeks out God personally in our circumstances. Faith believes that God has a plan and a purpose for every life; trust looks for God's activity in both the good and bad seasons we experience. Faith believes the Bible is truth, not a collection of hypothetical stories; trust tries to actively apply scripture to our lives, even when it places us in contrast to culture or popular opinion.

The Temperature Of Trust

One of the greatest stories of trust displayed during a gap between a problem and a solution is found in Scripture in Daniel, Chapter Three. It is the story of three guys—Shadrach, Meshach, and Abednego who were part of the population of Israel taken captive by the King of Babylon when Israel was conquered and defeated. Along with their friend Daniel, Shadrach, Meshach, and Abednego were serving in the royal palace as wise men and advisors to King Nebuchadnezzar.

As they were serving, the king constructed a giant golden statue of himself. This massive monument stretched ninety feet into the air and could not be missed by anyone. An order went out: "People of all races and nations and languages, listen to the king's command! When you hear the sound of the horn, flute, zither, lyre, harp, pipes, and other musical instruments, bow to the ground to worship King Nebuchadnezzar's gold statue." This was not a decree to be ignored, as it concluded with the warning, "Anyone who refuses to obey will immediately be thrown into a blazing furnace."

This decree put these three men in a gap between a problem and a solution. They knew in their hearts they could not worship the golden statue of the king because their God commands them to worship no other gods but Him. They knew they were going to have to stand up for what they believed in, even if that put them in danger of death. As the band begins to play, people begin to bow—all but Shadrack, Meshack, and Abendigo. These three put their faith in the God of Israel who commanded them to worship no other gods. They stay true to God almighty.

They knew their stance was a risky one, but their faith was worth the risk. The stance did not go unnoticed. "Some of the astrologers went to the king. There are some Jews, Shadrach, Meshach and Abednego . . . they pay no attention to you. They refuse to serve your gods and do not worship the gold statue you have set up."

To say that King Nebuchadnezzar was furious would be an understatement! He demanded these three men be brought in front of him. The three stood before the king as captives who had been blessed with great favor and honor. (They had been put in charge of an entire province of Babylon.) As the king questioned them, asking if it was true that they refused to bow down and worship his statue, they answered honestly. They knew the punishment for taking this stance was a fiery death, yet they stood by the God they had put their faith in.

The king offered them one more chance to bow to his statue in worship. They again refused. Their refusal is a testimony of the trust built upon faith. "O Nebuchadnezzar, we do not need to defend ourselves before you. If we are thrown into the blazing furnace, *the God whom we serve is able to save us*. He will rescue us from your power, Your majesty. *But even if he doesn't*, we want to make it clear to you, Your majesty, that we will never serve your gods or worship the gold statue you have set up."

These three men had faith in God's ability. They were committed to trusting in Him, whether He chose to save them or not.

> Their trust was not dependent on what God did for them. It was built upon what they believed He was capable of doing for them.

This was radical trust on display.

Radical trust can stir up strong emotions in those who lack trust. King Nebuchadnezzar did not understand the trust of these three because he lacked his own faith in the God they spoke of. He wanted these men to worship him the way they worshiped their God, and when they refused, he ordered the temperatures of the furnace increased seven times. The fire was so hot, the guards who had tied the three up and pushed them into the flames died when the doors were opened.

This is one of those stories I remember hearing in Sunday School classes growing up. It was told through old school flannelgraphs and coloring sheets of three smiling men getting ready to walk into the fiery furnace. The expressions on these kid-friendly materials did not match the emotion and seriousness of the story I heard. When we overlook the emotions involved in a scriptural story, we fail to appreciate the journey between a person's faith and his or her trust.

Take a moment and put yourself in the sandals of Shadrack, Meshack, and Abendigo as they took those first shaky, slow steps toward the flames licking the furnace doors. Think about the feelings that must have welled up inside them when the heat from the furnace flared against their skin. Imagine the terror and trepidation they must have felt the moment they saw the guards next to them fall dead as they approached the flames.

These three men had to travel a gap between their bold stand of faith and God's divine intervention. Here is a critical part of this story: God did not protect them *from* entering the flames. Rather, He chose to provide protection for them *in* the flames. They had to have trust to face the fire. It was into the furnace where God sent an angel to be with them and protect them. When King Nebuchadnezzar looked in, he saw four men instead of three walking around inside the fiery furnace.

The trust it took to face the fury of the furnace was great. Yet, think of how much greater that trust must have been as they walked out of the flames without even a single hair on their heads scorched by the flames!

Learning to trust God in this way not only transforms who we are, but it also transforms those who witness our trust. Most of us are not faced with the dilemma of stepping into literal fires in our gap seasons; however, each of our individual in-between places challenges us to not just have faith in who God is, but also to trust in what He does or does not do in our spaces of struggles.

Trust Personalizes

It is easy to claim faith in the easy times. When life is going well and we face no serious struggles, it's easy for us to praise God. We proclaim the goodness and grace of our Heavenly Father when we are basking in his blessings. It is much harder to worship God when our trust is tested. When we face an unknown future, have to deal with what seems to be an impossible problem, receive news that breaks our hearts, or have to mourn the end of an important relationship . . . these are times when our faith proclamations are tested, and we must test our trust in God's plans and purposes.

Psalm 9:10 tells us, "Those who know your name trust in you, for you, O Lord, do not abandon those who search for you." (NLT) Those of us who are facing a gap right now can cling to this promise. God will not leave you nor abandon you during your difficulty. When you allow that truth to permeate your heart, then you will truly be able to commit to personally trusting God in your gap.

When I first stepped out to go into ministry, I quit a full-time job with benefits to focus on building a women's organization, which I felt God calling me to start. At the time, my husband's income alone supported us, and on paper, the numbers never added up. Month after month, we trusted God to fill in the gap between our budget and our income. I remember one extremely tight time that transformed my faith in God's ability to provide into trust that He would always provide personally for us.

With a family of six, it can be a challenge to keep enough food in our house to feed our growing crew in the best of times. We had some unexpected expenses come up during this time, which meant we needed to really pinch our pennies in every area, including the pantry. After a week of creatively stretching our limited grocery supply as far as I could, I reached the end of our food with several more days until payday. I remember tucking the kids into bed that night with full tummies and just praying that God would provide something for breakfast.

I literally bent down onto my knees in my kitchen and opened the pantry door and prayed over it. I did the same thing with the refrigerator and the freezer. I planned to stay up all night praying for a miracle. I had faith that God could provide. I had read all the stories in Scripture where he provided food and had heard many people testify how God showed up in their time of greatest need. However, I found myself wondering if he would show up for us.

About midnight, I felt the Holy Spirit whisper to my heart at that moment. "Trust me. Go to bed and rest." I felt fear as I lay down to sleep that night, but my body was exhausted. I fell asleep praying, "I have faith that you see me and hear me. God, I am trusting you to move."

A few hours later at about 6:00 a.m. someone knocked on my front door. A friend from church was standing there with groceries in hand. I looked at her in disbelief and all she said was, "The strangest thing happened to me last night. God told me around midnight last night to get up early today to go buy you groceries."

That carload of meats, vegetables, fruits, and even some of my children's favorite snacks personalized my faith in God into a deep trust that He hears me, He sees me, and He cares about my needs.

I am not alone. Many people have found their faith being personalized by their struggles to trust God in their gap. The homeless person who has faith that God is real but has to wrestle daily with trusting that God will provide for his basic needs of food and shelter. The person who lost their job and has faith that God sees her need but is struggling to trust that God will open new doors and help her not fall behind on her bills. The addict who has faith that God can help him overcome his temptation but has to trust for strength in the face of each fresh temptation. The parent that has faith that God can work in the life of her prodigal child but has to trust God to let her loved one hit rock bottom. The family member that has faith God gave him a loved one with special needs as a gift but must trust in God to provide wisdom and direction for support, treatments, and provision. A child that has faith God loves him but is trusting that He has a forever home for him or will bring him home to a healed household one day. The individual that sits in the doctor's office, hearing a hard diagnosis who has faith that God can heal but must trust in God's will for her own illness. The couple that has faith that God hears their prayers to give them a baby but wrestles with trusting God each month when tests come back negative. The person with the faith that he will see a loved one he is grieving but wrestles with trusting God to comfort his aching heart and direct him into an unknown future without this person's presence.

As the writer of Hebrews said, "Faith in God is the willingness to believe in what you cannot see." Faith is choosing God. It is the opening of our minds to who God is and how He desires to move in and through us. Faith is a decision to accept His love, grace, and forgiveness in our lives. Trust, however, is the translation of the mental choice to believe into a heart condition, to apply the promises of God to our decisions, our relationships, our motivations, and our gaps. Our faith becomes personal when it is transformed into trust, a process that stretches us in countless ways.

The Tension Of Trust

While each gap is unique, they all have something important in common—the tension our gaps create between our current level of trust and the level of trust God wants us to grow into through our struggle. There are three common places where we experience the tension of trust in the gap. They are our sight, our comfort, and our control. As we discuss each of these, think about your own gap and how you might be experiencing a tension between faith and trust in these areas of your struggle.

Our Sight

Often the length of our view determines the depth of our trust. The further we can see into the future and the clearer that view is, the more we are inclined to trust in someone or something. However, since our gaps are often full of twists and turns, which obscure our vision, there is an inherent tension between our desire to see what is coming and the need to trust God blindly.

Each of us experiences our gaps from a personal point of view. We focus on how we feel, and we are impacted by the struggles of this season. We have our own vision of how we would like to be released from our struggle. We have a mental picture of what we would like our "happily ever after" to look like. The problem is, our vision is shortsighted and based on our wants and desires. Our personal vision often places us in a tension to trust God's expanded, eternal view of our gaps. Our Heavenly Father sees not only how our journeys through the gap impact us but also how they influence others around us. The God of the gaps sees what our struggles can create in us and others because he has an expanded, eternal picture of our struggles.

King Nebuchadnezzar was transformed by watching the trust of Shadrach, Meshach, and Abednego in action. The king saw these three men enter the fires full of trust in their God, and he saw them exit the furnace alive and unharmed. Seeing this example of bold trust transformed his heart, and he cried out, "Praise to the God of Shadrach, Meshach, and Abednego! He sent his angel to rescue his servants who trusted in him." Nebuchadnezzar then decreed that anyone who speaks a word against the God of Israel would be torn limb from limb and their houses turned into piles of rubble. He boldly announced, "There is no other god who can rescue like this."

Our gaps are full of blind spots:

We can't see every person our gap is impacting.

We are not able to picture how our gap will end

We struggle to imagine how our future will look.

We can't visualize God's solution to our struggles from where we stand.

The tension is to trust in God's promises and His presence, even when we cannot see His activity or the path He is carving out for us to take through the gap.

Our Comfort

Our human nature is to pursue what is safe and comfortable and avoid that which could stretch and strengthen us. If we are honest, most of us use our security instead of our faith as the determining factor for many of our daily decisions. Most of us cling to the edges of our carefully cultivated comfort zones with white knuckles and exhausting grips.

Gaps, by nature, are not comfortable, cozy places. Like a natural disaster, they often slam into our comfort zones, leaving little recognizable trace of the way things were before. Gaps disrupt our fiercely guarded comfort zones in every way imaginable:

They change how we spend our time.

They reorganize our priorities.

They reframe our definitions of health, happiness, and success.

They force us to make choices that impact our sense of security and stability.

They challenge us to have tough conversations that have been long avoided.

They force us to risk reputation and relationships during necessary decisions or changes.

They require us to be humble and ask for help from others.

This reshaping of our comfort zones in our gaps leads us to live in a constant state of tension between our longing for comfort and God's use of our struggles to stretch and develop the depth of our trust we have in his will and his ways.

Our Control

Proverbs 16:9 wisely reminds us, "In their hearts humans plan their course, but the Lord establishes their steps." (NIV) The human heart longs for control of our present struggles and our future successes. In our humanity, we plan, prepare, and plot carefully calculated courses throughout our life. We believe our ways are the best ways, so we pursue them with focus and drive. God, with his eternal wisdom and perspective, is often offering us divine detours, invitations to journey toward his purposes rather than our plans. However, many of us decline or ignore these opportunities because to travel God's way would force us to sacrifice our feeling of control.

For some of us, the pursuit for control is what led us straight into a gap. While others end up in a gap that was neither chosen nor deserved. No matter the role that control played in your gap, both cause tension because our desire for control is in opposition to the inability to control the people, circumstances, or timelines that often shape our gaps.

We cannot control how another person feels.

We are not able to control decisions of others that impact our future.

We are not able to control how bodies will respond to treatment.

We cannot control how much we will be charged for medical or legal help.

We cannot control the length of our struggle.

We cannot control other people's opinions or reactions.

We cannot control God's activity.

Trust is hard. It is important we stay focused on Jesus' command to each of us in John 14:1, "Don't let your hearts be troubled. Trust in God, and trust also in me." (NLT). Learning to trust in God's ways also requires us to trust in something else . . . His timing.

6

Willing to Wait

One of the hardest aspects of the gap for me is the pace. Some days seem to fly by faster than I want as I try to savor every moment. However, most days feel like they move in slow motion and time is dragging by. The slow seasons involve so much waiting, and I do not enjoy waiting—at all.

In the gap, I found myself waiting more than I had ever had to wait before. I had to wait on other people to return important phone calls with vital information. I had to wait for appointments that always seemed to get scheduled further away than I had hoped. I had to wait for scheduled dates. I had to wait to adjust to new, unfamiliar schedules. I had to wait for decisions to be made. My gap was full of bursts of activity, followed by long, drawn-out seasons of waiting.

I had faith that God had a plan and a purpose for our struggle, and I trusted that He had not abandoned me. Yet, I still *desperately* wanted our struggle to pass as quickly as possible. I had no desire to linger in the gap. The majority of my prayers those early days revolved around the timeline of our gap as I pleaded with God to speed up processes and bring a quick closure to our circumstances. I begged, bargained, and demanded Him to move faster. At times, I was even so bold as to tell God how quickly this could all be over if He would just do this, this, and that. I boasted that I could end this gap faster then He seemed to be capable of doing.

In God's personal love for me, He knew my weakness for waiting. Out of his great grace for me, I believe he orchestrated a very poignant lesson in the early days of our gap. This lesson has forever changed the way I view the struggle to wait in the gaps we face, and I hope it helps you reframe some of your thoughts as well.

The Waiting Room

Two of my children had been struggling with chronic strep throat, and the doctor who was caring for them recommended they both have their tonsils removed. He thought it would be easier to schedule their surgeries on the same day and time, allowing them to recover together. The morning of the surgeries, we arrived at the hospital to get them prepared for these routine procedures. Both of the kids were feeling anxious and fearful. I did my best to soothe and comfort each of them as they were admitted, dressed, and settled into a shared pre-op room to wait until the nurses came to take them to surgery.

When that moment came, we prayed together, and I kissed each of them as they were wheeled into the operating room in parade formation as I was escorted out to the waiting room area. I found a seat and waited. I prayed as I waited for each of them, for their procedures to go smoothly and without complication. As I sat staring at the beige walls of the waiting room, my mind began to wander to the circumstances of our gap. I found myself reciting the mantra in my mind that I had been repeating to God for months. "God, please bring a close to this quickly. Hear my cry God and move to end this situation for us now!"

As I paced in the waiting room that morning, the Holy Spirit began to speak to my heart and mind. I realized that no matter how impatient I was while waiting to be reunited with my children after their surgeries, I would never—not in a million years—storm through the sterile doors of the operating room and demand the doctor hurry up. I could never, ever imagine taking the scalpel out of the doctor's highly trained and qualified hands, thinking, *I can do this faster than you and better than you. Get out of my way!* To do either of these things would be crazy and irresponsible!

I was perfectly content to wait for a skilled surgeon, a stranger, to work on each of my children. I was comfortable with them being behind closed doors and out of my reach because I knew it was for their good. I trusted in his skill and his timing, even wanting him to take all the time he needed to ensure he completed the operation properly. A huge wave of conviction washed over me as I realized. . .

With God, I was not content in the waiting room. I was storming through the operating doors, constantly demanding He work faster. I was proudly trying to pry the "scalpel" out of His heavenly hands as I claimed my ways were better and faster.

> I was more willing to wait for a doctor to work on my children than I was willing to wait on God to work in my gap.

I was granted a divine perspective that day, and it changed everything about my outlook on our struggle. Later that afternoon, as both kids were sleeping off the anesthesia on the couch, I whispered these words in prayer: "God, I am sorry. I am sorry that I have been more focused on my comfort than on what you are doing through these difficult circumstances. I am sorry I have been demanding you to move faster. From this day forward, I will trust not only in your ways but also in your timing. I am willing to wait for you, God. I will wait as long as you need me to for your purposes and plan to be accomplished."

Let's be clear. I still do not enjoy waiting. But this powerful lesson cultivated in me a new willingness to wait that I did not have before. I still have urges of wanting to storm the gates of heaven for expediency. When I wrestle with those feelings now, I visualize those doors to the surgery area and remind myself that God is working on something behind the scenes that I cannot fully see or understand right now. I have tried to be a student of waiting and how to do it better as the months have turned into years in our gap. One of the stories that taught me more about God's use of waiting rooms was the story of Lazarus.

Gaps That Glorify

In the book of John, we read the story of another waiting room, this one involving Jesus and three of his close friends, Lazarus and his two sisters, Mary and Martha. Lazarus had become very ill in his hometown of Bethany, so his sisters sent an urgent message to Jesus. "Lord, your dear friend is very sick." (John 11:3, NLT) However, Jesus did not immediately run to Lazarus's bedside to heal him or ask Father God to heal his friend from afar. Instead, he said to his disciples, "Lazarus's sickness will not end in death. No, it happened for the glory of God so that the Son of God will receive glory from this." (John 11:4, NLT) He and his disciples stayed for two more days where they were (outside Bethany) before Jesus finally said to them, "Our friend Lazarus has fallen asleep, but now I will go and wake him up." (John 11:11, NLT) The disciples were confused. They assumed that if he was only sleeping, he would get better on his own. Jesus clearly corrected them, saying, "Lazarus is dead. And for your sakes, I'm glad I wasn't there, for now you will really believe. Come let's go see him." (John 11:14, NLT)

Two days. Two days where Mary and Martha paced the floor of the waiting room, hoping for a miracle. Two days likely taking turns stepping outside the house, staring at the horizon, hoping to see Jesus approaching the house to heal their beloved brother. Two days wondering if their message had arrived and what was taking their Lord so long.

Then the moment came. Lazarus drew what seemed to be his final breath. The sisters watched as the illness won and claimed the life of their brother. They prepared him for burial during the first day by binding up his hands and feet and wrapping cloth around his head and face. He was laid in a tomb, and a great stone was rolled in front of it as was the custom burial practice of the day.

Mary and Martha were no longer waiting. They were mourning. Friends, neighbors, and family came during the days following Lazarus's death to comfort and console the two heartbroken sisters. Four days into shiva, the Jewish week-long period of mourning, one of these friends tells Martha that Jesus was on his way. Martha leaves the house and goes to meet him outside the village. When she sees him she cries, "Lord, if only you had been here, my brother would not have died." (John 11:21, NLT)

Martha's feelings are understandable. She believed Jesus had the power to heal her brother, and she felt strongly that *if* he had come, then Lazarus would still be living. Many of us can relate to Martha in this moment because we have thrown similar questions at God when our own time of waiting ended in disappointment or pain. We cry out to God and ask why He did not move and heal our loved ones, restore our relationships, bring back our children, provide needed resources, make a way for a dream to happen, or break the power of an addiction.

Most of us have uttered our own versions of "if-then" statements to God at some time during our gaps. *God IF you would have _____ then _____ wouldn't have happened.*

What is (or was) the if-then statement you use with God in your gap? Are you allowing that statement to define and limit your relationship with God? He did not answer in your time or your way so you feel entitled to be angry, resentful, or disappointed in Him? Sadly, many people allow this kind of reaction to draw a line in the sand between God and themselves, pushing away from Him instead of continuing to trust Him and seek out His purposes behind His actions and His timing.

Martha did not stop with an if-then statement. Her very next words to Jesus were not words of anger or condemnation but words of faith and trust. She said, "*But even now* I know that God will give you whatever you ask." (John 11:22, NLT) But even now. Those three words offer a powerful challenge to every person who finds themselves waiting impatiently on God to act or struggling to accept the timing in which He has or has not acted. The words *but even now* reveal the unspoken words of her heart, a heart broken by the loss of her brother. *I still have faith in who You are, and I trust You even though Lazarus is gone.*

I challenge you to stop for a moment and consider how you can apply Martha's model of faith and trust in your own gap. Simply take a moment to personalize and complete this simple prayer:

> God, it is hard to wait in this gap. I am tired, even weary. I have struggled to understand Your ways and Your timing. But even now _____.

I do not know how you filled in the blank of that prayer, but I trust that if you were honest and real with it, it will be a step toward growth in the gap. If you needed to tell Him that you are angry and frustrated, He will love you and be there for you. If you needed to tell Him you are hurt but still committed to hanging in there, He will love you and be there for you. If you needed to tell Him you are recommitting yourself to trust Him in this season of waiting, He will love you and be there for you. There is no declaration we can make that will drive Him away. He loves us and is there for us—no matter what.

The story of Lazarus does not end with Martha's powerful proclamation of faith to Jesus on the outskirts of town. Jesus did not come to comfort her in her pain but to convince others through her pain that He was the Son of God. Nothing—not even death—could limit the power of His Father in Heaven!

Jesus had Martha, who had already gone to get her sister Mary, and the gathering crowd take him to the tomb where they had lain Lazarus down. Jesus told them to roll the stone aside, and Martha began to protest, worried about the smell. Jesus looked at her and said, "Didn't I tell you that you would see God's glory if you believe?" (John 11:40, NLT)

Jesus then stood in front of the open grave and prayed to His Father in Heaven, "Father, thank You for hearing me. You always hear me, but I said it out loud for the sake of all these people standing here, so that they will believe You sent me." Then Jesus shouted, "Lazarus, come out!" (John 11:41–43, NLT)

Jesus knew that allowing Lazarus to die and stay in the grave for four whole days gave *God a divine opportunity to be glorified* when Lazarus walked out of the tomb fully alive and healed. He did not walk out of the tomb as a sick man but as a healthy man, one who stood as a powerful testimony to the power of God and the potential of his timeline.

Not every gap gets the unexpected plot twists and happy ending that Mary and Martha received. This stretch of waiting, which Mary and Martha had to endure, brought glory to God in one of the most powerful displays recorded in Scripture. It is important to note that our gaps still glorify God, even if they drag out or don't end the way we would want.

W.A.I.T.

The more that I studied the biblical concept of waiting, the more I realized how many Bible characters, like Mary and Martha, spent time waiting in a gap:

- Abraham waited years as an old man for a promised son to be born to him at last.
- Joseph waited in a Egyptian prision after his brothers had sold him into slavery.
- The nation of Israel waited to be set free from Egyptian slavary.
- Once free, the Isralites had to wait a generation before entering the Promised Land.
- Joshua waited as he circled the city of Jericho.
- David had to wait years after first being anointed to become King of Israel.
- Jonah waited in the belly of a whale for three days.
- Daniel waited in the bottom of a Lion's Den.
- The world waited hundreds of years for the birth of the promised Messiah.
- Jesus waited three decades in obscurity before starting his public, earthly ministry.

It was clear that as I wait, I rest in good company.

One day, I was sitting on my couch with my prayer journal. I wrote the letters W.A.I.T down the side and traced over and over the letters as I prayed for God to show me not just that I needed to wait, but how to do it better. I wanted to wait, but it was so difficult to be patient for a timeline I could not see or understand. After about an hour of praying and sitting in silence, a series of words came to mind. I realized each word corresponded to the four letters I had been tracing as I asked God for direction and better understanding. I filled in the words and stared at the message before my eyes:

W: Willingly

A: Await

I: Inspired

T: Timing

I believed God was speaking answers to my toughest question and showing me how to wait on him. I spent weeks examining each of these words individually to help me better understand their impact when put together in this context of waiting during our gaps.

Willingly

Willingness is giving consent. It is being ready. It is agreeing to conditions and giving personal permission for something to happen. Many of us who are thrust into a gap, do not consent to our struggles. Yet, there comes a point in our struggles where we have to choose to either avoid God or come to Him for direction and healing. A willing heart seeks to connect with God in the gap. A willing mind strives to understand God's wisdom and direction in the struggle. Willing eyes strain to see things from God's perspective, even in their pain. Willing ears listen carefully to God's word and prayerfully process it in the context of their personal problems.

In my gap, I stumbled upon a verse in Psalm 54, which helped me cultivate a willing spirit with God. "I will sacrifice a voluntary offering to you; I will praise your name, O Lord for it is good." (verse 6) This verse helped me recognize that in the context of my willingness to come to God, I was sacrificing my attempts to create my own escape route out of the gap. I was offering Him my willingness and consenting to His timeline, rather than pushing my own. David penned this Psalm out of a personal experience of disappointment and betrayal. His heart was hurting as he declared his willingness to sacrifice a voluntary offering to the God of his gap. God desires our willing surrender, but He will not force it or manipulate it. He waits for us to be willing. The other key part of this verse that spoke to my heart was that David was praising God by making this offering because the name of God was good . . . not because his situation was good.

The gap may be hard, but God is still holy. You don't have to like your situation to be willing to trust His heart and His ability.

Awaiting

Awaiting is a verb that identifies an individual currently engaged in the action of waiting. Even though waiting feels like a stretch of inactivity, awaiting God is not passivity. The "waiting rooms" of our gaps are often full of activities, such as planning, researching, talking, praying, hoping, crying, questioning, worrying, wondering, and pacing. In reality, waiting is an active, exhausting experience.

What are you doing while you wait? Keep this in mind as you wrestle to await God's timing: The emotions that God gifted us with are designed to be indicators of our heart, not dictators of our actions. In other words, we need to let our feelings draw us into conversations and connection with God, not determine our activity in the gap as we wait for Him to direct our steps. This does not mean we just sit and twiddle our thumbs while the world passes us by.. It means we seek out the right activities to engage in while we wait. Use our waiting wisely by engaging in conversations that help us grow in our understanding of God, care for our personal health, are healthy ways of coping with our emotions and stress, finding ways to serve others, and cultivating supportive community and relationships to support ourselves in the gap. Waiting is hard but it does not have to be wasted. Use this time in a way that helps you grow in your health, in your understanding, in your perspective, and your connection with God who is present with you in the wait.

Inspired

To say that something is inspired is to identify it as something of God or from God. To speak of inspired timing means acknowledging that God uses time—both seasons of activity and seasons of waiting—for his purposes. Proverbs 16:9 speaks to this concept. "We make our plans, but the Lord determines our steps." Consenting to God's timing means being willing to follow His direction and His pace for our steps. In our gaps, one of the hardest truths we have to wrestle with is that God's inspired timing not only orders our steps but also ordains our stops.

Timing

The prophet Isaiah captures this powerful message from the Lord and shares it in the forty-ninth chapter of his namesake book, "At just the right time, I will respond to you. On the day of salvation I will help you." Our right time is seldom God's right time. Isaiah 55 again declares God's voice, "My thoughts are nothing like your thoughts... and my ways are far beyond anything you could imagine. . ." God's timing is eternal and takes into account more factors than we can conceive. If His timing does not line up with our timeline, there is a reason. Being willing to await *His* inspired time means consenting to stay in the gap until just the right time that He is ready to respond, move, or act.

This concept of W.A.I.T. has been formative and powerful for me in my gap. I pray that by sharing these perspectives with you, it helps you to consider what your waiting room looks like right now and how willing you are to trust God in places for unknown lengths of time.

Waiting is hard. Period. There is no making light of the struggle that we experience in the waiting rooms of our gaps. I know waiting is not easy. There are still days where I wrestle with my own level of willingness to continue to wait. However, just like each of these examples that I have shared with you, our willingness to wait is often one of

God's greatest platforms to show His power and remind us of His sovereignty.

I do not know your story, but I know God. He promises us He has a plan and a purpose for our lives, even the seasons of waiting. The results of our waiting can be bigger than anything we could have imagined. I urge you to be willing to trust in God and in His timing during this time of struggle in your life.

My fellow gap traveler, please know I understand that time in the waiting room is not easy. I ask you to cling to this truth during your difficulty: God promises us that if we are willing to wait, then He will give us strength for the struggle.

7

Strength to Struggle

Educators, psychologists, and marketing specialists all understand the power of repetition. They know the more we are exposed to a concept, the more we are inclined to understand it and internalize it. Teachers review material over and over to help students understand it better and remember it easier. Advertisers intentionally create catchy jingles that get stuck in our minds long after the ad has stopped playing on our televisions or in our Facebook feeds, in the hope that our forced familiarity will translate into sales and profits for them.

Growing up I absorbed many of the repeated words and phrases spoken around me, often in a church environment. Without effort, I memorized key scriptural verses I heard used over and over in lessons and sermons.

The lyrics of popular hymns still run through my mind at the most random of times from the years of singing them week after week. I can recite the Lord's Prayer by heart, not because I set out to memorize it, but because I heard it repeated so many times in my youth. There is no doubt that repetition is a powerful tool that helps us to internalize information!

I am sure you are wondering why am I sharing this with you and how it applies to the gaps of our lives. The truth is that many of our gaps are filled with the repetition of common *Christian* catchphrases, which often get absorbed into our minds and hearts and begin to shape our thinking and behavior in the gap. Some of these comments are positive and can be encouraging, while others are hard to hear:

I will be praying for you.
God works all things out for his good.
God is not done yet.
Claim victory over this battle.
Struggle will make you stronger.

There is one phrase I heard over and over in the gap, one I have a particular disdain for. I cannot tell you the number of times that well-meaning people would send me cards with this "motto" emblazed in gold glitter on the front. I lost count of the number of people who would hug me awkwardly and then repeat this phrase to me before walking off, not knowing what else to say. I am guessing if you have spent any time around Christians in the gap, you have probably heard this phrase a few hundred times as well: "God will never give you more than you can handle."

Ugh! Even typing it out makes my blood pressure rise a few points.

Consider this chapter both my personal theological soapbox and my battle cry to wage war on this dangerous untruth that has become an accepted statement in Christian circles. I want to share with you how I became aware of my own absorption of this statement and the dangerous impact it had on my gaps, how different my gap journey became when I replaced this untruth with God's power, and how finding freedom from this often repeated and accepted phrase could dramatically change your perspective on your gap and God's role in it.

Weariness Wake Up

A few weeks after the waiting room lesson, I woke up one morning and decided to go for a run. It is important for you to know that this was not a normal occurrence in my life. On this morning, the last time I had gone for a run on purpose was more than a decade prior during an assigned mile-long run in gym class.

This particular morning, I was out of shape and had zero experience or training in running. I laced up the only tennis shoes I owned (my mowing shoes) and started out the door. I didn't stretch. I didn't drink water. I didn't think about where I was going. I just went.

I started out jogging in our neighborhood, and since I felt pretty good running *downhill*, I made a mental commitment to run about a mile-and-a-half to our church and back. I determined I could do anything I set my mind to. At the start of this "workout," running three miles did not seem ridiculous. The error in my thinking *quickly* became apparent when I reached the bottom of the long hill and began to feel a searing burning in my legs and pain in my chest. I knew I *should* stop but I was *determined* to not give up.

I stubbornly pushed myself a full mile-and-a-half. I made it all the way to the church where I collapsed on the front steps. I had nothing left. I was totally out of strength. I was embarrassed at how out of shape I was and did not want to admit I was wrong or not strong enough. So I sat there for a long while.

Hitting this level of physical exhaustion also made me realize my soul was just as tired as my body. Even though I had told God I trusted Him and was willing to wait on His timing, I realized I was still trying to face the day to day events of my gap under my own power. My strength was gone, and I was worn in the very depths of my spirit.

Much like on the run, I had just pushed my outer strength to completion. I had also pushed myself far beyond my own inner strength. That realization made me feel like a failure. Too tired to walk home, I pulled my phone out and texted my husband to come and pick me up. Over the next few days, I tried to make sense of the overwhelming sense of guilt that had come over me after my run.

Then it happened. I saw a friend who knew about my gap at the grocery store. I could tell she was uncomfortable and did not know what to say to me. We engaged in small talk for a few minutes, and then she gave me a hug and said, "Well, we know that God won't give you more than you can handle, right?" Somehow, hearing that phrase yet again collided with the questions I had been wrestling with since my run. A cosmic connecting of the dots moment happened in my heart in the middle of the produce aisle.

I realized I had heard that statement so many times during difficulties that I had come to believe it as truth. As I headed home, I pondered how the constant repetition of that phrase had led to me to developing a sense of responsibility to be strong in my struggle.

In the weeks that followed, I dug deep into scripture and made some freeing discoveries. I confirmed that these words that had been shared with me countless times, "God will never give you more than you can handle." are found nowhere in Scripture. Yet, it feels as though Christians have grafted these words onto the gospel and spoken them with the same level of conviction that I had heard when talking about the red letters of Jesus.

I realized this phrase is one of the greatest lies the enemy of our souls has whispered into generations of believers to fill us with pride, shame, and self-reliance. He has used this seemingly innocent phrase to cultivate a culture of Christians who push away from God in times of hurt rather than running to Him to help us through our struggles.

I understood just how much this mentality had developed within me. I had felt obligated to handle my day-to-day problems alone, forging the stubborn mentality, which said, "If God gave this to me, I should be able to handle it by myself. I don't need help from Him or anyone else." I had to process that feeling that I was letting God down because I believed He expected me to be able to handle my situation under my own strength. No where does Scripture promise us that our struggles will *never* exceed our strength. Just the opposite! We were designed for dependency! Our troubled times drain our human strength quickly and put us in a posture of needing to come to God for help.

Surrender To Strength

For me, help came most often from God's Word. Prior to this massive undoing of my sense of having to struggle alone, I often engaged with Scripture out of routine. I would follow a reading plan to have just a few bites of wisdom to take with me through the day. However, being in a place of complete weakness taught me to rely on God for strength each day. In that place of dependence on Him, I developed a craving for God's Word.

When I felt weary, afraid, unsure, tired, or scared, I could pull out my Bible and open it up and find comfort and strength. It was soothing to sit and let holy promises refresh me like a cool drink on a hot day. I had never approached God out of hunger, nor habit. Surrendering to this place of need allowed me to find a connection with His heart, His presence, and His Word like never before.

Over the years in our gap, I have found that God often allows us to endure more than we can handle to pull us closer to Him as we seek Him for strength. In our weakness:

He wants us to come to him and ask for help.

He wants us to seek Him for direction.

He longs for us to surrender our problems to Him.

We cannot overwhelm God by giving Him too many problems.

We cannot overextend God by giving Him something too big or too hard.

Here is the perspective-changing truth that every gap traveler *must* grasp and cling to:

> No matter your struggle, you can never give God more than He can handle.

Our gaps may drain our strength, but they will never drain God's strength. When we are weary and worn out, God is there to carry us through our seasons of struggle. When we feel exhausted and depleted, the Holy Spirit who lives within all believers, ministers to us and infuses us with God's strength and power. From cover to cover, Genesis to Revelation, Scripture boldly declares the power and the might of God. I was amazed to discover that the promise of God's strength is a constant thread woven throughout *every* book of Scripture. From beginning to end, His Word promises that the strength of God will sustain the children of God in the face of any hardship or trial this world will bring our way. Here are a few of the promises that have upheld me and continue to give me the strength to struggle forward each day through our gap:

- "Do not be afraid or terrified because of them, for the LORD your God goes with you; he will never leave you nor forsake you." (Deuteronomy 31:6)

- "For the Lord has driven out before you great and strong nations. And as for you, no man has been able to stand before you to this day. One man of you puts flight a thousand, since it is the Lord your God who fights for you, just as he promised you." (Joshua 23: 9-10-11, ESV)

- "Look to the Lord and his strength; seek his face always." (1 Chronicles 16:11, NIV)

- "Wisdom and strength belong to God; counsel and understanding are His." (Job 12:13, HCSB)

- "He renews my strength. He guides me along right paths, bringing honor to his name." (Psalms 23:3, NLT)

- "Each time he said, "My grace is all you need. My power works best in weakness." So now I am glad to boast about my weaknesses, so that the power of Christ can work through me." (2 Corinthians 12:9, NLT)

- "May you be strengthened with all power, according to His glorious might, for all endurance and patience. . ." (Colossians 1:11-12, HCSB)

This is the strength that is available to us in our struggle! The strength of God that is proclaimed from cover to cover in The Word of God is also promised to the people of God in their times of need. God does not hoard his strength. He offers it freely to all who believe in Him, and no matter how much we bring to him, we will *never* find the end of God's strength or capacity to handle anything we bring to Him!

Letter Into The Gap

My fellow Gap Traveler,

I know you are tired and worn out. I know you are exhausted by decisions that need to be made and conversations that need to be had. I know some days, it takes all you have just to open your eyes to your current reality and choose to get out of bed and face another difficult day. I understand.

I know you have been told to stay strong, hold it together for other people, and you will never be given more than you can handle. Believe none of it. I know the friends and family who spoke those words into you meant well, but they did not know each of those statements added to your burden of feeling the need to perform well in your worst moments. You wear the mask of strength and try to project a powerful presence when in reality, you are coasting on fumes.

You do not have to be strong. It is okay to admit you feel weak and worn out. Please hear my heart. I know it is scary to lean on someone else for strength or admit you need support, but no matter how hard you try, you cannot go through the gap under your own power. Yes, you may try to draw strength from other things for a while, but no substance, human relationship, or physical activity can sustain you, and in the end, those things often leave you more depleted than before.

Other things may motivate you, but they cannot strengthen you. There might be people who you want to be strong for or accomplishments and milestones you want to achieve. While those are great, they are goals on which you focus your activity, but they cannot fuel you for the fight on their own. There is only one source of strength that can sustain you for the duration of the struggle—the power of God.

If you have engaged with Him before, lean into Him now. Dust off your Bible and reconnect with his heart and his voice. Trust Him to not only guide your steps in the gap but to strengthen them as well. Dig into His Word out of need and hunger. Draw power from His promises and His presence.

If you have never connected with Him before, choose to now. Stop struggling under your own limited strength; allow His endless strength to sustain you. No matter the struggle you face, there is nothing too big (or too small) for your Heavenly Father to handle! All that is required to connect with the strength of God during your struggles is a conversation with Him through prayer. A humble, simple whisper of, "I can't do this on my own anymore, God. I need Your help and Your strength" is all that you need to unleash His energy and ability into your gap and experience His power personally.

Converting Promises

Physicists define energy as *the ability to do work*. They separate energy into two categories: potential or kinetic. These categories describe the activity level of the object. An object with potential energy is in a position to become active, whereas an object with kinetic energy is active already.

For example, a marble balanced at the top of a ramp will sit in a state of potential energy as long as it remains unmoved. However, if someone were to give the marble a nudge with her finger the marble's energy would be instantly converted from potential to kinetic as it is set in motion down the ramp. Now, imagine the same marble/ramp scenario, but this time with a spiritual twist.

Imagine that the marble balancing at the top of the ramp represents the Bible. How many of us have a Bible that spends more time on a shelf than in our hands? It's words of truth and comfort remain unseen because we're either too busy or too prideful to open its pages. So it sits, full of promises that go unread and unclaimed in our circumstances.

God's Word is packed full of potential! Comfort that has the potential to bring you assurance when you are struggling. Strength that has the potential to uphold you when you are weak. Truth that has the potential to change your eternity if believed. Characters whose lives have the potential to influence and shape your own life. Perspective that has the potential to change your view of the world around you and knowledge about what your purpose is in it. Promises that have the potential to change your trust in God and how He may be using your problems.

The Bible is not just a book of words to be read but a record of promises to be claimed and applied to our circumstances and our struggles. Through the pages of scripture, God whispers promises to his people; He promises to love us, fight for us, strengthen us, sustain us, uphold us, be with us, use us, and redeem us.

However, simply reading His promises does not unleash their power. Much like the finger that nudged the marble into action, something must activate the power of God into our gaps. That is the role that prayer plays in our struggles. Prayer is the activator of God's promises in our problems.

8

The Language of the Gap

Prior to the gap, my prayer habit was cold and impersonal. I had heard sermons that taught prayer formulas and outlined formats to use to make sure all of the "right" things were said during prayer time. Those teachings helped me organize my lists to bring to God on a regular basis into clearly defined categories—praise, confession, gratitude, and requests. If you want to understand what my prayer time with Jesus looked like, put down this book and go to YouTube and look up "Coffee with Jesus" (the clip with the actor in a blue shirt). Watch this two-minute and twelve second-long skit, and see if your prayer life has ever looked like mine before I entered the gap.

Can you relate? This was the type of prayer "routine" I brought with me into my gap. However, studying the prayers of several well-known biblical characters helped to reshape my view of prayer and radically changed my own prayer practices. I hope that in sharing what each of these characters taught me about prayer, it will help you to examine the role prayer is playing in your gap.

David: Personal Prayers

The first biblical character who helped change my perspective of prayer was David. The pages of Psalms in my Bible are tear-stained and heavily highlighted because on hard days, I often seek perspective from David's intimate conversations with God.

Scripture gives us a pretty clear picture of David's life. We know that his early years were spent tending to the flocks of his father's sheep in the countryside. Then one day, his quiet existence was upended when a prophet named Samuel came to visit, in search of the next king of Israel to anoint. God makes it clear to Samuel that David is the one that he is to anoint. From that moment forward, David's life course is changed. Rather than hunting animals that preyed on his flocks, he slayed giants who taunted God's army. Instead of playing his harp outdoors on a hillside, he played privately inside the chambers of King Saul. His reality was no longer peace and comfort. Conversely, he became familiar with struggle and hardships.

David became a successful military leader who fought many battles to defend his country. He worked hard to respect the current reign of King Saul, yet the paranoid ruler grew increasingly jealous of David's victories and schemed to kill the young warrior. David was forced to live on the run, seeking refuge in caves and strongholds that dotted the countryside. Through all of this, he experienced the deep heartbreak of loss of relationships and friendships. David experienced firsthand what it was like to be unjustly accused and pursued.

After becoming king, David still had shortcomings and struggles. He made mistakes and committed sins. He mourned the death of his children. He was betrayed by those closest to him. He was not allowed to fulfill his ultimate dream to build a temple for the Lord.

David spent a great deal of time in different kinds of gaps.

David's words throughout the Psalms show us the desires of his heart. He longed to see situations from God's perspective. He had a deep desire to see God's plans and purposes come to pass through his struggles. He trusted God to strengthen him and protect him. He loved God and praised him, even when he was hurting.

King David is often referred to as "a man after God's own heart." His prayer life molded and shaped his heart and mind. Through prayer, he learned to wait and trust his Heavenly Father. By praying his way through his gaps, he walked hand in hand with God through every hardship. His prayers strengthened each step through his struggle. David understood that through prayer, he drew nearer to God and God drew nearer to him. No request was too small or too great for him to come to God in prayer. David prayed with purpose, passion, and persistence because he understood the privilege and power of prayer. David prayed his way through each gap. There are literally hundreds of prayers in the Psalms, but I want to share with you three of the most impactful to me in my gap.

Prayer #1:

In Psalm 27, David cries out, "Hear me as I pray, O Lord. Be merciful and answer me! My heart has heard you say, 'Come and talk with me.' And my heart responds, 'Lord, I am coming.'" (NLT)

I am a parent to four amazing children. I love each of them fully and completely. One of my favorite things to do is sit on the porch swing at our house and ask one of them the simple question, "What is new in your world?" The answers that come never cease to amaze and enthrall me. I learn about new hobbies, new friends, problems they are having at school, dreams for their futures, and emotions over struggles they face. I have made it clear to my children from day one that I am interested in their lives—all of them. I want to laugh at the small stuff with them as much as I want to cry about the big things beside them. They are my children, and I love them. That love motivates me to want to be involved and present in their lives as much as they will allow me to be.

That is the same way God feels about you.

The God of the universe, who hung the stars in their proper places in the night sky and molded the mountains with his bare hands, is your Daddy God. He created you and cares for you as one of his precious children. He longs to have the kind of personal relationship with you where he can whisper, "What is new in your world?" and you will open up to him about all things great and small in your life.

Prayer #2:

"I am praying to you because I know you will answer, O God.

Bend down and listen as I pray. Show me your unfailing love in wonderful ways . . ."(Psalm 17: 6–8, NLT)

David understood that prayers are deeply personal. They are an outflow of our relationship with God. It is one thing for you and I to stop what we are doing and listen to God's direction, but have you ever imagined what David is describing in this passage? Have you ever stopped to consider the implications of the fact that your prayers change the position of the Creator of the universe? When you pray, He bends down to pay attention to your pleas. When you call out to Him, He stops what He is doing to focus on you. Our prayers change the proximity of God, drawing Him closer to us and our struggles.

In that closer position, God doesn't just listen, He acts. He embraces His hurting children and comforts them. He may not choose to calm the storms we face, but He will calm us through the storm. Our prayers are an invitation for God to draw near to us and move in our hearts and our minds. Many times, as we face our gaps, we will discover that God is more interested in what is going on inside us and around us. Humbling ourselves in prayer opens a door to allow God to develop our faith, strengthen our trust, adjust our attitude, change our perspective, focus our thoughts, and grow our courage. Our prayers move the heart of God, and then He begins to work on our heart.

Prayer #3:
"Let all that I am wait quietly before God, for my hope is in him.

He alone is my rock and my salvation, my fortress where I will not be shaken.

My victory and honor come from God alone.

He is my refuge, a rock where no enemy can reach me.

O my people, trust in him at all times.

Pour out your heart to him, for God is our refuge." (Psalm 62: 5–8, NLT)

There may be lots of reasons we avoid prayer or struggle to come to God in our gaps, but I think at the heart of all of them is the misconception that prayer is performance. We feel like we must have the right words, spoken in the right order so that we may convince God to be moved on our behalf.

Prayer does not work like rubbing a genie out of a bottle. There is no magic formula for getting the God of the universe to fulfill our every dream and desire. Prayer is not meant to be a means to an end but a part of the journey we take with God through our time here on Earth.

What motivates you to pray? Is it a desire to make your life better and get what you want from God? If so, then you are missing the major point of prayer.

> Prayer is not about what we get by doing it. Prayer is about who we get closer to through doing it.

Our prayer time is our personal, private time with God Almighty. The more we engage in prayer, the more time we spend in His presence.

We miss out on the understanding that prayer is not a one way conversation where we tell God what we need from Him. Prayer is designed by God to be a two-way conversation. God does not desire for us to pray to Him out of routine. Rather, He wants us to come to Him because of our relationship with Him. God invites us to open up our hearts and share anything with Him, and God desires the chance to respond to our needs.

Nehemiah: Prayer Response

Nehemiah is another Old Testament character. He, along with thousands of others, was taken from his home in Israel into exile in Babylon where he was elevated to service to the king as the cupbearer. One day, his brother and some other visitors, who had already returned to Jerusalem, came to visit Nehemiah. They shared with him how the city walls were broken down and badly damaged, leaving the city vulnerable to attack from nearby enemies. Nehemiah felt a deep burden to return to his homeland

and help rebuild the city walls. His response to this heart tug is to spend time fasting and praying for confirmation, direction, and favor.

When our circumstances seem dark and desperate, prayer is the spark of hope we strike in our souls. Times of great problems should be times of greater prayer. However, many of us pray and expect *immediate* action from God. We believe that as soon as we say "amen" and open our eyes, our problems should be solved *right away* by God's goodness and grace. In Nehemiah's case, it took about four months for God to make a way for him to approach the king for permission to return home to address the condition of the walls and lack of security.

Once permission was granted, Nehemiah made the journey back to Jerusalem and surveyed the damage himself. Once he developed an idea of the project, he set out to accomplish this task in record time, organizing the people for maximum efficiency during the build.

However, not everyone was happy about this undertaking. There were enemies that came against this project and tried to find ways to undermine it, slowing its progress. One day, when all of the main sections of the wall were completed, two of the enemies sent a message to Nehemiah about wanting to meet with him. He returns his own message saying he is too busy working and can't meet with them. Ever persistent, these two send four more invitations to Nehemiah to come and meet with them, and each one is declined by Nehemiah. Finally, the enemies send a servant to come and read aloud fabricated accusations against Nehemiah in front of his workers. Nehemiah's response in that moment is powerful. "They were all trying to frighten us, thinking, 'Their hands will get too weak for the work, and it will not be completed.' But I prayed, 'Now strengthen my hands.'" (Nehemiah 6:9, NIV)

Here Nehemiah was working to rebuild the walls of the city while in constant danger from those who did not agree with his actions. He faced a moment of weariness and frustration and the constant opposition to his efforts, and he responded in prayer. Nehemiah did not pray that God would change the hearts and minds of those who stood against them. He did not pray that God would silence their opposition or the taunting. He did not pray that God would rain down fire and lightning and destroy his enemies. He did not pray for God to send angels to assist in the building efforts to speed up the efforts of reconstructing the walls of Jerusalem. Instead, he prayed a simple, faith-filled prayer asking the God of inexhaustible strength to make his hands strong enough to continue to be faithful to the work he had been called to do.

This simple prayer has become my life verse. In fact, I had the reference tattooed on my wrist in the darkest days of our gap to serve as a constant reminder to go to God in prayer . . . that His help is only a breath away. Learning to pray that God would strengthen my hands for the gap I am in has molded my prayers to stop asking Him to spare me and to start asking Him to sustain me. Having the courage to pray for sustaining strength and submit to our gap seasons serves as a powerful catalyst for God to move through our struggles to strengthen our relationships with Him.

> Nehemiah's prayer for strong hands reminds us all that our hands are always strongest when they are folded in prayer.

Nehemiah's first reaction to the distractions others threw at him was to pray. For many of us (myself included), that is not always our first reaction. Often, when we discover we are in a gap, our first reaction is to try to do everything we can to fix it or solve it ourselves. We talk to people, we manufacture plans, we stress out, and we lose sleep. Then, when nothing is working and we become more desperate for a solution, we pray.

Do you struggle with this?

Do you wait to come to God in prayer until you have tried everything else?

For many, it is pride that keeps them from hitting their knees. For others, it is the fear of what God may say or do if they come to Him that keeps them from seeking Him. Some struggle with feeling unqualified to talk to God because of sin or shame in their past or present. Others are angry at God for their struggles and blame Him for their pain, so they refuse to go to Him with a need. Many simply believe God is too busy with wars, epidemics, miracles, and other "big problems" of the world for Him to be bothered with their small stuff. Do you identify with one of these emotions or justifications when it comes to crying out to God in your gap?

Our struggle with self-sufficiency not only drains us of our strength, it often silences our prayers. Instead of going to God early in our struggle, we wait until the problem feels big enough to bring to God. Those of us who struggle with this often have a cold, formal view of God and how we should pray to Him. When we fail to grasp the privilege of prayer, we often fail to understand the power that prayer has. One of the greatest tragedies of faith is when a believer fails to understand or engage regularly in personal prayer with his or her Heavenly Father.

We cannot be prepared for all of the twists and turns of the gaps. I like to describe Nehemiah as a pray-pared (from *prepared*) person. When the unexpected happened, he did not react out of emotion but rather, he responded out of prayer. He sought to please God, not people . . . and often relied on prayer to pave the way for him to bravely follow the places where God led him.

Jesus: Pray For Others

The sections of Jesus' life that are documented show how highly he prioritized the practice of prayer. Many times, after spending time with the crowds teaching, he would retreat off by himself to talk to his Father in Heaven. He also often prayed in public, thanking God for His activity, praising Him for His ability, acknowledging His power, and asking God for wisdom and direction. Prayer was part of a natural rhythm for Jesus.

In addition to modeling prayer, Jesus often taught on the topic of prayer. He taught the crowds The Lord's Prayer in his Sermon on the Mount. He implored followers to pray boldly and continuously. He encouraged believers to be stubborn knockers who name their needs with God again and again. He made it clear that prayer is a privilege for those who have faith in God, and engaging in prayer has the power to move mountains, heal the sick, make the lame walk, and cause the blind to see. One of his most difficult teachings about prayer can be found in Luke 6:28 where Jesus says, "Bless those who curse you! Pray for those who hurt you."

Ouch.

It is one thing to pray for yourself, for those you love, or those who are disconnected from you. It is a much more challenging thing to pray for those who have hurt you throughout your gap journey. Most gaps involve some kind of people pain—people who have let us down, people whose words caused pain, people who betrayed us, people who walked away from us.

Jesus practiced what he preached. As he hung on the cross, he cried out a prayer, not for himself but for those who had cursed him and brought him pain and unjust punishment. He prayed aloud, "Father, forgive them for they don't know what they are doing." (Luke 23:24, NLT)

Learning to pray for those who have hurt us and forgive those who have wronged us is one of the most difficult lessons we will face in our seasons of struggles. It's a topic that needs more than a few paragraphs to unpackage, so we will spend the next chapter talking about how to follow these challenging red letters in our individual gaps.

9

The Fight to Forgive

told you in the beginning of our time together, that this was not a book about me or my journey. I have aimed to share with you in a way that centers the focus on the lessons and perspectives God has taught me as I have lingered in a difficult gap, one which has grown and deepened my connection with Him. I know we have tackled some tough topics already in our time together— faith, trust, waiting, emotions, and prayer. The conversation we are about to have may be the most difficult one yet.

We need to talk about forgiveness. The very fact that I am bringing up this subject may frustrate and anger some of you. I get it. I know that the very mention of it may tempt some of you to close the book and walk away at this point . . . I understand. If you will stick with me and keep reading, I think you'll be surprised *just* how much I understand.

Here is the thing: I am a big believer in never telling someone to do something that I am not willing to do myself. So for that reason, I am not going to use this chapter to tell you how to forgive. Rather, I am going to share with you my story of my struggle to forgive. I am choosing to share in this way not because I am an amazing example, but because I am willing to be gut-level honest about how hard this part of my gap has been for me. I hope you will indulge me in this chapter to open up with you and share some more of my story with you. This particular piece of my story all began on a Sunday morning, about a year into my gap.

Red-Letter Wrestling

"Then Peter came to him and asked, 'Lord, how often should I forgive someone who sins against me? Seven times?'

'No, not seven times,' Jesus replied, 'but seventy times seven!'"

The sermon in church that morning was on Matthew 18. Hearing those red letters from Jesus read aloud hit me like a ton of bricks. If I'm honest, they made me angry. I kept trying to apply the command to the context of my gap, and I just couldn't do it.

A person, *THIS person,* who had caused me so much personal pain in my gap and could still hurt me and cause me pain . . . *yet*, there is an expectation for me to forgive them over and over and over? How is that fair?

I wanted to stand up and walk out of the church but was afraid of what people would think. I wanted to argue and plead my case for why this passage seemed one-sided and unfair, but I knew this wasn't the place or the time. So I sat in the pew and stewed in my frustration and silent protests. When the service ended, I exited the church quickly, taking my questions, struggles, and anger with me. I spent the day—and many days that followed—venting to God in prayer and conversation.

I was honest with him, explaining I felt entitled to my anger, hurt, and pain. I reminded Him that the circumstances we had endured were unthinkable. It was one thing to forgive someone over and over for small offenses, but things this big, this painful, this life-altering . . . surely Jesus could not have meant to forgive this!

I gave Him names of people whose actions were unjust, unfair, and in my mind, unforgivable. In doing so, I drew a line in the sand. As far as I was concerned, these people were off limits for Him to ask me to forgive. I simply could not and would not forgive *these people* for the pain and hurt that they had caused. I felt like the severity of my gap must somehow be exempt from this call to forgive, especially repeatedly. I considered the matter closed and off limits for further discussion.

The weeks that followed were strained. My connection with God seemed off.

Every time I engaged with Scripture, I avoided passages that would speak to forgiveness. When I talked to God in conversation, I was silent about my struggle to practice forgiveness. I felt myself slipping back into more carefully calculated interactions with Him, ones I could control.

I didn't like the feelings I was having, so I changed my approach. Instead of ignoring the command to forgive, I decided I would argue my case as to why I couldn't do it. Why I shouldn't have to do it. While searching for a holy loophole out of this merciful mandate, I kept running into roadblocks. I ran smack dab into Mark 11:25, "But when you are praying, first forgive anyone you are holding a grudge against, so that your Father in heaven will forgive your sins, too."

Not only am I told to forgive someone who caused unthinkable pain, but my own forgiveness is contingent on my obedience to this rule? God, this is not fair!

I switched Bible translations and collided with this powerful proclamation in the Message version of Matthew 6, "In prayer there is a connection between what God does and what you do. You can't get forgiveness from God, for instance, without also forgiving others. If you refuse to do your part, you cut yourself off from God's part."

Ouch.

I knew what God was directing me to do. I just didn't want to do it.

I became stuck in a secondary gap between God's call to forgive those who hurt me and my strong, stubborn desire to cling to my anger and bitterness.

I camped in this place for months.

During this time while I had my heels dug in, I experienced a heaviness in myself. I felt it as I went through my day. I felt it as I interacted with people. I felt it when I connected with God in prayer, study, or worship. I felt it when I was alone. The more I avoided the call to forgive, the heavier the burden became.

Finally, out of desperation, I cried out to God honestly and simply, "I don't *feel* like forgiving." In the silence that followed that statement, the Holy Spirit whispered a thought into my mind.

Forgiveness is not a feeling. It's a choice.

I knew right then that if I waited until I felt like forgiving, I would remain stuck in a spiritual neutral zone forever. So I prayed and asked God to guide me.

Journey To Release

Nothing changed overnight, but I was not avoiding the subject of forgiveness anymore, and I was praying for God to change my heart and my perspective so that I could choose to take steps of obedience along the path of forgiveness.

My breakthrough came a few weeks later.

I was reading *The Weight of Glory* by C.S. Lewis, and I stumbled across this line that knocked me to my knees: "To be a Christian means to forgive the inexcusable because God has forgiven the inexcusable in you."

I was broken.

Suddenly, a rush of memories came flooding back to me, a slideshow of my mistakes and mess-ups. Each one, no matter the size or severity, had been forgiven by God and covered with His grace and acceptance. Even the worst pieces of myself—those which I still wrestled with guilt over—were forgiven and pardoned by God's love.

Never does God draw a line in the sand and declare certain acts or certain people beyond the scope of His love. Never does God declare that a sin or struggle is too big for Him to forgive. He does not withhold His grace from anyone or any situation.

> I suddenly realized that God will never ask us to forgive someone more than He has forgiven us.

I was overwhelmed, convicted, and challenged all at once.

I sat down and made a list of the people whom I had once declared out of bounds for me to forgive, and I prayed over each name. I was honest with God about my perceptions of each person and the role that they had played in our gap. I spoke with full transparency with God about the emotions that each name stirred up in my soul. In the midst of all that honesty, something prompted me to pray a prophetic plea that became the catalyst for change in me. I said, "God, I need to learn to see these people through Your eyes and Your heart. Please help to change my perspective of them. Please help me be released from the impact of these strong negative emotions that I have toward each of them."

This practice became a routine during my struggle to release and forgive. When I would encounter one of these people, through a reference or direct contact, I prayed that same type of prophetic plea. *God, change my heart and my perspective toward them.* It was through this persistent prayer and a life-changing visit to a Florida beach that God taught me the most powerful lesson about how to choose forgiveness.

Lessons In The Sand

A speaking trip to Florida was just what my heart and soul needed during this leg of my gap journey. My soul was weary from wrestling with struggle for forgive. My intentions were good and my prayers were heartfelt; however, I had not found this strength or peace in myself to declare a pardon once and for all to those who had hurt me and my family.

Sitting on a beach, near water is always where I feel closest to God. So the natural outpouring in that moment of intimacy with my Heavenly Father was prayer. I told him that I was tired of fighting and tired of carrying around so many hard feelings.

I felt the need to name those feelings in writing all of the sudden. I grabbed a stick and I began to engrave on the wet sand these words:

- *Sin*
- *Bitterness.*

- *Anger.*
- *Guilt.*
- *Hate.*
- *Hurt.*

I stared at these words, which had been limiting me. Like a small pot trying to contain a growing root system, these strong feelings had been limiting my growth and holding me back from moving forward fully. These barriers had boxed me in, and I became stuck in this space until I found the strength to break through them. As I stared at them, I felt a desire within myself to not be defined by this list any longer.

"God, show me what to do to move forward."

Then something amazing happened as the tide began to creep closer.

A few letters at a time, the waves began to wash away the words I had written. It was not instantaneous. There was not a singular wave that came all at once to create a blank slate. Rather, it was piece by piece, letter by letter, wave by wave. I stood there watching with tears in my eyes because I had finally found the understanding to forgive.

I felt immediately released from the expectation I had that forgiveness had to happen all at once. I realized I had still been waiting for this big, lightbulb-like moment when I would suddenly not *feel* angry or upset anymore, and then I could choose to extend forgiveness. Yet, forgiveness is not a one time act! It is not choosing to forgive once and for all. It is choosing to engage in an ongoing process of releasing.

Ongoing because we are human. We are not wired like God to forgive and to forget. We remember. Each memory that gets brought back up, unleashes a fresh ripple of emotions and struggle into our hearts and minds.

As I watched the last letters disappear from the sand, I thought of my journey over the last few months. I began to appreciate that each of my prayers for perspective was like a cleansing wave of washing over my soul. Each time I was willing to wrestle with the call to forgive was a fresh wave of strength sustaining my struggle. Each time I was willing to be honest about my emotions was a wave of truth eroding the weight of my hurt and anger on my soul.

After I left the beach that day, I wrote one sentence down in my prayer journal as a takeaway and reminder: *I will forgive at every remembrance of the hurt.*

Personal Process

After I returned home from my trip, I sat down with a cup of coffee and a stack of stationary. For several hard hours, I composed letters to people who I had been praying over for months. People who I had been asking God to change my perspective toward. I did not condone their actions or try to sugarcoat the impact their choices had on me and those I love. I was honest with them about how they had caused pain, even though they might never fully understand. Most importantly, I expressed that I was choosing to release myself from the anger I had carried toward them. I was choosing to lay my resentments down and not be weighed down by them any longer. I was choosing to forgive.

There was power in putting those sentiments into writing.

There was power in sealing and addressing envelopes.

However, there was still fear in dropping them into the mail slot.

I knew that to communicate the words meant I had to be accountable to the actions those words might produce. I knew it was not going to be easy, but by sending those cards, I was committing to myself to not only express forgive once but to fight to live in forgiveness going forward.

I released the letters and took a deep breath. A new chapter in my story began.

Following Forgiveness

As I I write these words, it has been almost eight years since I dropped those letters into the mail slot.

Has it been easy? No.

Have I struggled? Yes.

A few weeks after mailing the letters, I saw one of the individuals at a restaurant. Initially, anger welled up inside me. But I was able to remind myself that their presence was not going to rob me of enjoying a meal with a friend. I excused myself and took a moment to remind myself of all I had processed and prayed through. I felt the anger lessen as a sense of peace settled over me.

That first face to face encounter taught me something critical—boundaries in relation to forgiveness. When we choose to forgive, we must also be wise and discerning as to what level of relationship and contact that person needs to have in our lives moving forward.

> Forgiveness is not an eraser for the past. It is a catalyst for change in the future.

I honestly did not have any personal connection to this person prior to their involvement in the circumstances surrounding our gap. There was no reason to pursue personal connection outside of my expression of forgiveness with this person. That day in the restaurant, I did not speak to this person or go out of my way to acknowledge them. I did smile at them when they got up to leave, making eye contact with me for just the slightest second. I could tell something in my heart had shifted through that first encounter post-forgiving.

There were others with whom I had to make peace with, those whom I did have a longer-lasting personal connection. There were people I was going to continue to see and interact with for much of my life whom I had to prayerfully ask God to guide me in setting new boundaries and learning how to walk in grace and wisdom at the same time.

One of these individuals whom I interact with regularly is the person who has done the greatest damage and inflicted the greatest pain on me and others. At the time of this writing, this person has never indicated any level of regret or remorse for their words and actions. Early on, I saw this behavior as prideful, and it infuriated me. Over time, I have come to understand that forgiveness is still something I can walk in and choose, even if the other person doesn't ask for it or deserve it. Forgiveness is a personal choice that I alone am accountable for, no matter the circumstances.

As I prayed for wisdom for how to move forward with this individual who had hurt me so deeply, yet was still a part of my life, I came across a quote from Warren Buffett that resonated with me. In fact it spoke to me so powerfully that I wrote it on a piece of paper and have had it hanging in my office for years: "Always take the high road, it is far less crowded."

Forgiveness does not mean I must assume the position of a doormat, but it does mean I have to hold myself to a higher standard. I must be more intentional with my words and my actions around this individual because the temptation is always great. I have coupled Buffett's advice about the high road with the wisdom of Proverbs 3 to form a common prayer that I often utter before I engage with hurtful people in my life. It often sounds something like this:

> *God, I know that you have called me to forgive this person and walk in forgiveness with this person. I trust you to protect my heart and guide my actions. I lean on you*

for understanding and direction. Help to guide me to the high road, not out of pride, but out of healing for there I will find both protection and strength. Show me the steps I need to take.

I heard someone once say that the act of forgiveness is one of the most Christ-like things we do as humans. I have experienced the truth of this statement over and over. Choosing to forgive at every remembrance of the hurt has given me a better understanding of the love of Christ. For me, I have to fight to forgive because it inherently goes against my self-preservation instincts as a human and puts me in an uncomfortable position. Christ doesn't have to fight to forgive us. It comes naturally to him.

Some of Jesus' final words in human form came as he hung horrifically on a wooden cross. Each breath he took required effort, and the words he spoke through his crucifixion were few. But he was intentional to speak words of forgiveness to those who had placed him there. With his dying breaths he spoke forgiveness. His example of forgiveness was one of the factors that caused a Roman soldier to utter, "Surely this was the Son of God." (Matthew 27:54)

When we are willing to forgive and walk in forgiveness toward others, people take notice. Forgiveness is a powerful picture of the gospel at work in the heart and life of a Christ follower. It is one of the greatest outward expressions of our inward wrestling and changed perspectives. In fact, to some who watch our choices and the changes in our behavior, the act of forgiving another person may be one of the most powerful exposures they to the love of Christ in action.

Reflection

So there it is, my honest story of my fight with the concept of forgiveness and my daily battle to walk in forgiveness at each reminder of past actions and events. I do not present myself as an example or a standard—far from it. I simply share my experiences in hopes you can relate to my honesty. It is my prayer that as you ponder my story, you will also reflect on your own. To be honest, it is hard to fully heal and move forward in your gap without walking the path of forgiveness. I encourage you to take some time before moving to the next chapter to use these questions as points of prayer and conversation between you and God:

1. Do you view forgiveness as a feeling? How does it change your perspective to think of it as a choice?

2. Is God asking you to forgive more than He has forgiven you?

3. Have you prayed for those who have wronged you or hurt you?

4. Have you viewed forgiveness as a one-time act or an ongoing process you have to engage in?

5. Who is God calling you to forgive in your gap?

10

The Choice to Hope

One of the Old Testament prophets whose struggle I connect with is Jeremiah. Here was a guy born into a priestly line with an expectation that he would spend his life performing sacrifices in the Temple of the Lord. However, God's purpose for him did not line up with the expectations of his family or community. God had created and called Jeremiah to be a prophet and to speak bold truth to hard hearts. Jeremiah's willingness to proclaim God's words landed him a life-long gap that included prison, exile, homelessness, and being thrown to the bottom of a deep muddy pit. Through his obedience to God, Jeremiah's control and comfort were wrecked.

One of the most relatable passages of Scripture I have discovered and connected with in my gap is Lamentations

3. It is believed this chapter was penned by the prophet Jeremiah as he cried out in frustration to God about his gap. It is full of raw emotions, which Jeremiah named and used to connect with God in a real and authentic way. He was telling God that he felt as though God was picking on him and had made his life difficult. He was being honest about how he felt punished and singled out by God. In verses 1–20, Jeremiah powerfully describes some of the feelings he wrestled with, many of which I can relate to. I encourage you to open a Bible and read the full passage for yourself. Here are a few of the statements that he makes:

"He has led me into darkness, shutting out all light." (v.2)

"He has buried me in a dark place, like those long dead" (v. 6)

"He shot his arrows deep into my heart." (v. 13)

"Peace has been stripped away, and I have forgotten what prosperity is." (v. 17)

"I will never forget this awful time, as I grieve over my loss." (v. 20)

In verse 21, something shifts and Jeremiah writes one of the most captivating sentences in all of Scripture. This singular sentence is packed with so much power, we are going to break it down and talk about one piece at a time as we wrestle to apply it to our personal gaps.

YET

Before this word is used, Jeremiah detailed his struggle and his hard emotions. He was honest about how hard his life had become and how overwhelmed he felt in this gap. He was authentic about the degree of difficulty he was facing.

The first word of Lamentations 3:21 is one of my favorite words in all of Scripture. Every time I see this word show up, I pay extra attention to what is happening because something is about to change. The word by itself is nothing remarkable. It is three little letters. But the concept they represent is huge. The word is *yet*.

When you encounter the word *yet* in Scripture, it is often used to shift gears, change the narrative, or refocus the story onto something else. I call it a hinge word because like the door to a room, it is often closing down one thought and opening up a whole new conversation or concept. Which is exactly what is happening in Lamentations 3:21. With those three little letters, Jeremiah is making a brave declaration that despite all he has gone through, he refuses to wave the white flag of surrender or stop following God in obedience—YET.

I used all caps with this word because with these three little letters, Jeremiah is making a bold and captivating statement that his past struggle does not define his present or determine his future, YET. With those three little letters, Jeremiah is shifting his heart from *what* he has experienced to *who* he trusts in. YET.

YET is potential and possibility.

YET is faith and forward momentum.

YET is a courageous catalyst for change.

YET is perseverance under pressure.

YET is a reminder that Jeremiah's story is not over.

YET is a choice.

Like Jeremiah, we each have the same powerful choice available to us in the context of our personal gaps to declare YET in spite of our circumstances. I acknowledge that our individual struggles have been full of hurts and hardships. I know that our challenges have stirred up strong and complicated emotions, which we battle daily. I know there have been things that have happened to us that seem unfair.

So here's the deal: We can choose to park our minds in this place and fixate on what has happened to us, on what we have lost, or on how hard this journey has been **OR** we can choose to shift our mindset and declare YET! Take a moment to ponder this important truth: Cultivating a YET mindset does not diminish your experience or downplay your emotions. Instead, it courageously chooses to not define who we are today by our past.

This journey has been hard YET God is guiding me.

This gap has been long YET God is strengthening me.

This experience has hurt YET God is healing me.

This struggle has been exhausting YET God is refreshing me.

This circumstance has seemed unfair YET I trust in God's justice and timing.

This situation has been hard to understand YET I know God hasn't left me alone.

Prior to this hardship, I did not have a close relationship with God, YET I now realize how much I need His help, His wisdom, His peace, and His presence in my life.

What is the YET statement you need to declare?

I

YET is a personal decision only you can declare in your personal gap.

The second word of Lamentations 3:21 is the word "I." It stands as a reminder that no matter how much someone loves you, they cannot create a YET moment for you. I am underlining the word I in this verse because your parents, spouse, friends, children, family members, and loving neighbors can pray for you, but they cannot make a YET choice in the gap for you.

Out of His great love for us, God grants free will to each person He has created. He loves us enough to pursue a relationship with everyone. In His eyes, no one is ever too hurt, too stubborn, too sinful, too angry, or too far away for His love to be extended to you. He loved you enough to send His son, to lay down his life for you and in doing so, He chose you and declared you to be valuable to Him. He loves each of us too much to force us into a relationship with Him. One of the most loving things God does is give each of us the choice to accept Him or reject Him. We each get to choose for ourselves if we will connect with the love, grace, mercy, and hope God offers us through faith in Him.

Faith is personal.

Trust is individual.

YET must be chosen in your mind, felt in your heart, and declared with your mouth.

This gap is hard and I am struggling; YET I . . ._____
_____.

Only you can finish that sentence.

(Still)

I place the word (still) in parentheses as we talk piece by piece through this verse because it's use in this context implies a previous choice or condition. The word's use in this verse affirms Jeremiah's already existing faith in God and prior decision to obey and trust God. His use of it in this context declares that *though there has been hardship, it has not cancelled out my faith in you or my choice to serve you.*

For those of us who, like Jeremiah, were connected with Christ prior to our gap journey, this word holds the significance of continuation of connection. However, it is critical to stress that (still) does not imply sameness or stagnation. The gap will challenge and change how we interact with God and expand our perspective of how we view God's activity and presence. The entry point level of faith and trust that we have when we enter the gap will be challenged by the circumstances we face, the emotions we feel, the doubts we wrestle with, and the questions we ask. Our choices are to respond by pushing away from God or digging deeper with Him.

As I have shared throughout these conversational chapters, my **belief** (head knowledge) *in God* existed prior to my gap. My **relationship** (heart connection) *with God* was developed and deepened by seeking Him during my struggles. Yes, I have experienced a great ongoing struggle YET I (still) trust that God loves me and I (still) choose to trust Him, His word, His ways, and His timing.

I know there are many others who did not enter into the gap with faith but have connected with God in relationship through their difficult journeys. To you, I simply suggest reframing the use of (still) in this verse to reflect your experience. Simply slide this word to the front of the verse for you:

(Still) I have questions; YET I choose to connect with you God.

(Still) I have doubts; YET I ask you God to help my unbelief.

(Still) I have fears; YET I am going forward afraid and trusting you to guide me.

Ultimately, this word (still) serves as a reminder that we bring history into our gap with us. However, we must remember, it is not our previous choices but our present ones that define and direct our futures.

Dare

I am grateful for Jeremiah's use of the word **dare** in this powerful declaration because it recognizes the audacity and difficulty of shifting his focus from his hurt to his hope. I am putting the word **dare** in bold letters to honor the bravery of Jeremiah and each gap traveller who has also chosen to push back with faith against our circumstances.

The dictionary defines **dare** as *having sufficient courage: to confront boldly: DEFY.* Think about those words in the context of your personal gap struggle:

When have you needed sufficient courage in the face of your challenges?

What/Who have your struggles forced you to confront boldly in your life?

What odds or stereotypes are you defying as you move through the gap?

You see, to **dare** is to choose to engage and refuse to give up. I know your struggle is hard but your perseverance in this gap is a daring act! Take a moment to celebrate your own courage to keep going!

Hear my heart, I know there are moments in this struggle when our hands feel tied or we feel stripped of our power to change the circumstances we face. I wrestle with frustrations too when I feel I'm unable to take or control outward actions. However, I have learned that no matter the limitations of circumstances, nothing can limit God's ability in our gap! It's HIS ability, not mine, that gives me the courage to **dare** daily.

Yes, I have been through much-YET I (still) **have courageous faith that God is able**. . .

Yes, each day is a battle- YET I (still) **have sufficient trust that God is with me. . .**

Yes, the struggle is hard- YET I (still) **confront my circumstances in prayer**. . .

Yes, the future is unknown- YET I (still) **defy doubt and fear**. . .

To Hope

When I was in seminary, I had a hermeneutics professor who stressed the importance of context when understanding a word or concept in Scripture. He used a phrase, which has stuck with me. "Words are known by the company they keep." I appreciate this wisdom because I strongly believe great damage is done when Scripture is taken out of context. I think it's important we look at a verse, a story, or a concept and examine what is before it and after it so we understand it fully within the context it is found.

To fully understand Jeremiah's choice *to hope* in this verse, you must understand the backdrop against which it is set. Jeremiah is a prophet to the nation of Israel in a season where God's voice was not popular or welcomed by the masses. The king, the nation's leaders, and many of the people had abandoned God's laws and were worshiping the gods of other nations. They were trusting in their military to protect them rather than in God to provide for them. Jeremiah is one of the only voices urging them to turn their hearts back to God.

His prophetic words are met with disdain and attempts to silence him, exile him, imprison him, and ignore him. The voice of Jeremiah was not a popular one in his time, and it resulted in a great deal of struggle and hardship for him.

YET he (still) **dared** *to hope.*

I am putting this final phrase of this verse in italics to acknowledge the power of the choice *to hope* in the context of struggle. The apostle Paul knew the power of hope and he declared at the end of 1 Corinthians 13 that three things will last forever—faith, hope and love. He went on to say that of the three, love is the greatest. I fully agree, but I would also add that of these three powerful and enduring concepts, hope is the hardest to define.

How do you define hope?

While you ponder your answer, I will give you mine.

I believe hope is the derivative of a relational connection with God. As we grow in our trust of Him and His ways, we develop a confident expectation that no longer views our circumstances in the context of the here and now but rather through the long lens of eternity. I believe to hope is to face the future with the conviction that God's power is unlimited and through Him, our circumstances could shift at any time. I believe hope is a forward focus that influences how we engage with the world around us and how we respond to the struggles we face.

One of the passages of Scripture that I think most illustrates what hope in action looks like in our lives is Eugene Peterson's translation of Colossians 3:1–2 in *The Message*. It reads:

> *So if you're serious about living this new resurrection life with Christ, act like it. Pursue the things over which Christ presides. Don't shuffle along, eyes to the ground, absorbed with the things right in front of you. Look up, and be alert to what is going on around Christ—that's where the action is. See things from his perspective.*

This passage helped me clearly see that hope is the choice to shift our focus. Hope is being intentional to not focus on the earthly details of our gap but rather on the activity of God in our gap. This passage challenged me to evaluate where my attention was fixed and understand that hope is not a one-time choice but a perspective developed by choosing to look up again and again.

Hope chooses to look up from the impact of the diagnosis and focus on God's ability to heal and his promise to comfort us.

Hope chooses to look up from the pain of a broken relationship and focus on the wisdom of God to know which relationships need to be restored and which need to be released.

Hope chooses to look up from the details of a loved one's passing and focus on the promise that if there was a shared bond of faith, there will be an eternal reunion one day.

Hope chooses to look up from the amounts of the bills piling up on the counter and focus on God's ability to open doors for employment, provision, and wisdom to pay our debts.

Hope chooses to look up from the daily struggles of homelessness and focus on God's constant presence in our struggle and the peace that he offers us.

Hope chooses to look up from the temptation of addiction and focus on the strength that God promises to provide us in moments of weakness.

Hope chooses to look up from the disappointment of infertility and focus on God's promise to catch our every tear and listen to our every prayer.

Hope is the gentle nail-scarred hand of your savior lifting your head toward heaven in a loving reminder that this current pain, disappointment, hurt, and fear is seen by the God of the universe. In his great love for us, God doesn't just abandon us to suffer in the gap alone., He floods our gap with His presence and waits for us to look to him

Here is an important question for you to ponder in the context of your own gap:

> What is your source of hope right now?

True hope can't be in something. Authentic hope can't come from someone. Genuine hope only comes from connection with THE ONE. The God who loves you. The God who sees you and hears you. The God who promises to never leave you or forsake you.

Choosing to declare "YET I (still) **dare** *to hope*. . ." in the face of your struggles is brave and courageous. Hope will not restore everything to normal, but it will help give you the strength and direction you need to navigate a new normal in your present and your future.

11

Navigating Between Normals

What is normal?

Normal is the collection of the mundane moments of our lives. The combination of all the "little things" that may seem insignificant and unremarkable by themselves; yet, together they often define our existence and our enjoyment of life. Normal is made up of things like laughter at inside jokes, dinner table conversations about your day, silly songs sung in the car while running errands, tickle wars, spontaneous dance parties in the living room, snuggles during a movie, hand-holding while driving, stepping on Legos® in the dark, late night conversations, the smell of a favorite food cooking in the oven, a room full of loved ones enjoying shared moments together, fights over messy floors and unfinished chores, and a thousand other behind-the-scenes moments whose value is often underestimated until something happens and those mundane moments suddenly become memories you cling to.

No one fully appreciates normal until it is taken away, and often normal slips away in the blink of an eye with little warning or preperation. Our sense of security is often anchored in the ordinary and predictable pieces of our world, which means that a loss of normal often leaves us feeling vulnerable and unsafe.

While no two gap journeys are the same, there is common grief all gap travelers share. We are all grieving a lost sense of normalcy while we try to understand and accept a new normal in our lives. In fact, that may be the best universal definition for the gap—*the in-between place between grieving a lost sense of normal and adjusting to a new unexpected normal.*

Why am I talking about this at this point in our conversation? Because, if I am being brutally honest, the most challenging part of my gap journey has been the space and time after the drama died down, the dust started to settle, the hard conversations happened, and the reality of our *new normal* started to settle in. Over time, I noticed there was this unspoken expectation people around me seemed to have that things could go back to normal now. That enough time had passed, and I should be okay on my own; they could go back to their regular routines and previous engagements with me. One by one, people went back to their normal lives while I struggled to adjust to a life that was now anything but normal.

I share this hard part of my experience because I know I am not alone in this often overlooked part of the gap journey. It is hard to feel like the world around you is going on as if nothing changed while you are still struggling to adjust to your personal world being forever altered.

Many times people pick up books like this one in hopes that it will have the secret answer to solve their struggle and ease their pain once and for all. As they start to near the closing chapters, they expect to be fixed and no longer hurting. If that was what you were hoping for in this book, I am sorry to let you down. The truth is, you are not going to find a quick solution to your struggle in these pages or any other pages.

I know there are some of you who just read that sentence and thought, "That's not true! The solution can be found in the pages of the Bible!" Well, no where does the Bible promise us *quick* solutions. Rather, the Bible promises us that in this life, we will endure struggle but because of God's great love for us, we don't have to struggle alone. The Bible speaks of loss and heartache and declares that God is near to the broken-hearted. The Bible acknowledges that we are going to feel weak and weary, and it invites us to find rest in a relationship with Jesus. In fact, some of the most dominant themes of the Bible are struggle, heartache, loss, and pain.

Ya'll (I'm southern at heart), I am going to be honest and say something that may offend many church leaders: The church is often guilty of trying to normalize the healing process. We host twelve-week classes and label them, "Overcoming _____," "Finding Freedom From _____," or "Healing from_____." The truth is that no matter how amazing the class or the teacher, you are not going to fully overcome your pain, find freedom from struggles, or heal from any emotional, physical, and spiritual wound in such a short period of time. What happens in Week Thirteen? When participants are alone and still fighting negative feelings or facing temptations, they feel alone or abnormal. Many whom I have spoken with over the years felt like there was an implied expectation that they should be "fixed" by the time they finished such classes, and when they still experienced struggles, they dressed themselves in embarrassment or shame, feeling abnormal or broken.

We offer three-point sermons in attempts to streamline the steps to find peace or heal from hurts. These practical sermons can lead to large altar calls and emotional responses from people; however, what happens three or four days later when those same people have difficulty in applying those steps in their daily relationships or problems. Many people often feel like they are not "normal" because those simple steps did not solve everything for them.

Countless experts, many of them well-meaning pastors and Christian counselors, have identified steps and written books to talk about the *normal* process people go through as we grieve and heal. They suggest similar steps for people to take and in doing so often imply that by going through each of these "milestones," we should make *normal* progress to healing and in doing, so will be able to get back to *normal*. When people finish the book, leave the retreat, finish the seminar, or complete the workbook, they feel like they should be fixed.

All of this has led to a "microwave mentality" that says healing should happen quickly and immediately. We should be able to pray, and the results should be instantaneous. We should be able to forgive someone who hurt us, and the relationship should be restored immediately. We should finish a Bible reading plan, and our struggles should cease. We graduate from a church class, and we expect our difficulties will disappear.

I have lost count of the number of Christians who have left the Church because their personal timeline to healing didn't match the message they heard from the Church. When they passed the *acceptable* time of hurting, they started to hear phrases like:

> *You need to pray more.*
> *You have unresolved sin in your life.*
> *Your faith must not be strong enough.*

I call this toxic normalcy. The unhealthy expectation that every problem should have a quick solution that results in everyone being happy, smiling, and acting *normal* again quickly. The church is one of the worst offenders of spreading this messaging to the masses. We are great to love on people during the "expected" time of hurting, but once the struggle lingers on, we distance ourselves from them, and often they push away from the Church as a whole. God doesn't expect us to be fully healed to come to Him or be involved with Him, so why does the Church attach an expectation for people to engage, serve, or lead?

It is my personal passion that the Church should be a safe place for people to hurt, struggle, be tired, feel weary, and process pain. There should be no timetable on how long their healing process should take or what it should look like along the way. I realize this is a much bigger conversation than I can unpackage in a few paragraphs or even a dedicated chapter. It's another conversation for us to engage in on the pages of another book in the future.

More than anything I want you to understand my heart—healing is a journey not a destination. I want you to know there is no normal way to heal. There is no set timetable on grief. There is no perfect way to process pain. The goal of this book is not to fix your problems but to let you know you are not alone in your pain. As we get ready to enter into the last chapter of our conversation, I want you to know that I recognize your gap will continue after our time together is done. If you ever need to be reminded of that, you can always revisit any of these chapters at any point on your continued journey.

After you put this book back on the shelf, there will be some days that are good and some days that are hard. There will be days where you laugh more than others and other days where you will cry more than others. There may be seasons where each day feels like a battle and others where you are doing well for days, week, or months at time.

Your gap journey is yours alone. Over time, at your own pace, and in the context of your own relationship with God, your healing will uniquely unfold. Over time, you will realize that you have put some distance between yourself and the gap you are leaving behind. It often happens with little fanfare or celebration. Many gap travelers look around one day and discover that their lives have settled into a new rhythm and without intention or coaching. Without planning, a *new normal* has emerged in life, and they have quietly transitioned from struggling to strength.

You may move on and forward from this gap, but you will always take with you the sacred scars of this journey. Let's finish our time together by talking about celebrating our scars and not being afraid to share our struggles.

12

Sacred Scars

One thing that I have not told you is that I am a word nerd, which means sometimes I like to dig deeper into the history of a word to fully understand its meaning. At the beginning of this book, I defined a gap as *a space between two objects* and throughout our conversations, we have talked about how on our journey to adjusting to a new normal, we often find ourselves getting caught in "in-between places." However, there is one other important aspect of the gap that must be addressed, and it begins by understanding that the word gap is derived from the old English word *gape*, which means *something open wide*.

A wound is often described as gaping when the body has been opened up by serious injury that mandates medical attention for it to heal properly. Likewise, the entry point to our gap—the circumstance, the struggle, the heartbreak, the diagnosis, or the loss—could be compared to a wound that opens a wide divide between in our sense of safety, comfort, and normalcy. The emotional, relational, or physical wound we have been nursing on this journey may eventually heal. But it is important to remember that serious gaping wounds are ones that do not heal without leaving a scar.

Sacred Scars

Our time in the gap may fade over time to a tender memory. The truth is that the experiences from the gap never really leave us. They leave an impression on who we are, how we process, how we engage with people, and how we view future circumstances. You could say that our gap journeys forever leave their mark our hearts, minds, spirits, and sometimes our bodies forever.

I am not the same person today that I was when I entered the gap.

You are not the same person that you were when you entered the gap.

We have been changed by what we have gone through. We carry our memories and experiences with us, and they each become woven into our everyday existence. No matter the degree of visibility, the hurt we have experienced along our gap journey carries over with us in some form into any new seasons, new experiences, new relationships, or new adventures. The way we respond to any given present moment is comprised in large part of the lessons and experiences we have had in the past.

Just as the nerves around the physical scars on our bodies are always a bit more hypersensitive to exposure and contact, so, too, are the instinctive reactions when an inward scar is touched unexpectedly. Even days, months, or even years after our gap experience. Without warning or notice, something around us can trigger a memory within us that stirs up deep feelings and reminders.

You could be reminded of a scar when the familiar lyrics and melodies of a song bring back memories and emotions that catch you off guard. Sometimes, a smell will waft your way in a crowded room that reminds you of life before the gap. It could be a scene you see played out in real life or on a movie screen that instansiously transports your heart back in time. It might be a line in a book or a comment in a sermon that can surprise you and take your breath away. Pictures or announcements of someone else's life event may remind you of missed moments or missing people. Old photos found at the bottom of boxes might bring tears to your eyes. It could be a specific location that is hard to revisit once you have journeyed through the gap. A specific date on the calendar may not be significant to most people, but to you that date carries the weight of painful reminders of lost opportunity and hard experiences. Holidays that were once celebrated without worry can make you more cautious and careful.

These scars are tricky. However, they are also a gift, a sacred bond that prevents us from compartmentalizing our past and shutting it off from our future. I believe they are one of God's gracious ways of helping us remember the journey we have been on and the lessons He has taught us along the way.

Tender Touchstones

All throughout the Old Testament, we see that after a significant battle or difficult lesson, people would often pause and construct an altar to God to remind them of what they learned about God's character through the struggle. These altars were meant to serve as touchstones to teach future generations about God's faithfulness in both the good times and the gaps. I have come to view my scars and the memories of them as touchstones. When they are triggered, I try to process my reactions prayerfully and use the time of stirred up grief as an intimate opportunity to worship my God who has personally carried me through the gap and never left me alone in my struggle.

There are some touchstone triggers that I can anticipate, like the yearly anniversary of the day that my life was forever changed. I have learned over the years to give myself grace on this day and permission to grieve all that has been lost. I often spend some time alone reflecting not only on the hurts from all those years ago, but also on the healing and strength that has come in the gap overtime.

As you go forward, be mindful that your scars are a part of who you are now. Your tender touchstones WILL get triggered as you go into new seasons, new relationships, new conversations, new experiences, and even new gaps.

When those moments come—and they WILL come—focus on this truth:

> Though scars are painful, they are often the greatest reminders of the progress God has guided us on throughout this journey.

Celebrate Your Story

When I first started this project nine years ago, I never dreamed it would someday be shared with other people. You see, in a culture that celebrates perfection and teaches us to hide our weakness, cover up our scars, spin our struggles, and reframe our mistakes, being honest about the "hard stuff" we are going through is not common. Most people, especially in church culture, are encouraged to struggle in silence until they get to the otherside of the gap. Then they can share from a perspective of healing and wholeness. In doing so, our struggles become something we can claim victory over rather than a topic to engage in honest dialog about the painful process of moving on and adjusting. For me, these pages were my safe place, my way of processing the pain I was feeling and the lessons I was learning through it. I found solace at my keyboard; it was the one way that I could organize my racing thoughts and begin to make sense of all that I was experiencing.

However, I noticed something happening in the conversations I was having with people. Over and over, I found myself talking with people who were also experiencing heartache and struggle. As we talked, I often felt prompted to be vulnerable and authentic about my own pain and often share with them something tI had processed in writing out these pages. I started to realize that God was using the messiest and hardest parts of my life to connect into the life of others again and again.

I didn't like it.

It is much easier to brag about our strengths than to be honest about our weaknesses. However, the more opportunities I had to be honest about the lessons I was currently learning in my ongoing gap, the more I started to find the courage to be honest about my pain. I also discovered that when I was willing to share my struggle, I would make a connection with someone else that always drew us deeper than surface level. Our shared pain opened up doors and enabled conversations, which allowed me to share God's love and goodness like never before.

No, this was never intended to be anything more than a personal, private journal where I could be honest about the wounds I had suffered and my journey to finding healing and meaning. However, one of the most powerful lessons I have learned in the gap is this: *Everyone has a story and everyone's story matter. Every piece of our stories matter, our successes and our struggles.*

My greatest prayer for the legacy of this book is not that you connect powerfully with my story, but you discover God's presence and purpose in your own story. As you begin to connect with Him in your gap, I want to challenge you to be bold and courageous to share your gap with others. Be honest about your struggles and authentic about your pain. Do not cave to fear and feel the need to hide your struggles or cover up your scars.

A Courageous Challenge

Whenever I preach at my church or anywhere else, I always try to end each message with a challenge, something tangible for you to do in response to the conversation we have had together. The time we have spent together between the covers of this book are not exempted from a bold call to action, so here it is:

I want to challenge you to share your gap story and the way you have seen God move through it in your life. I want to encourage you to prayerfully process this challenge, and in time, take to social media and post something real and genuine. Resist the urge to hide the hurt, cover up your scars, or polish over your pain. Be authentic.

Share your struggle.

Share how your faith has grown or developed through the journey.

Share your waiting rooms.

Share what you have learned about God through the gap.

You never know how your story may impact the life of another person who reads it. Your story may give someone else the strength to keep going in their own struggle or to seek God in their gaps. Your story may inspire someone else to find the courage to speak up and share their own experience. Your story may remind someone they are not alone and there is help and hope. You will never fully know the potential power of how God wants to use your story to impact the world around you until you entrust it to Him and are willing to open up.

I want to invite you to post your gap story using the #GodoftheGapsChallenge hashtag so that with one click, you and so many others can be reminded that we do not struggle alone. Each story we share will be unique to the traveler. As we read them may we all be reminded that we are united in similar shared experiences, emotions, and adjustments.

While no two gaps start from the same beginning, share the same experiences, or end up in the same destination, every gap is seen, heard, and valued by a loving God who is always one whispered invitation away from flooding our gap with His love, peace, wisdom, and presence. He is and always longs to be the God of every gap we face.

Bible Reading in the Gap

Genesis 22	Psalm 73	Matthew 14
Psalm 4	Isaiah 35	Matthew 16
Genesis 37–50	Psalm 84	John 8
Psalm 6	Isaiah 40–43	John 11
Exodus 1–2	Psalm 86	John 14
Psalm 9	Isaiah 49–51	John 15
Exodus 13:17– Exodus 14	Psalm 91	John 16
Psalm 12	Isaiah 52–55	Matthew 20
Exodus 16	Psalm 116	Matthew 22
Psalm 16	Isaiah 56–57	Luke 19
Deuteronomy 6-8	Psalm 118	Luke 21
Psalm 17	Isaiah 61	Luke 22
Deuteronomy 9–11	Psalm 119	Mark 15
Psalm 18	Jeremiah 29–31	Mark 16
Joshua 1	Psalm 121	Acts 3–4
Psalm 21	Jeremiah 32–33	Acts 9
1 Samuel 16–17	Psalm 126	Romans 3
Psalm 25	Lamentations 3	Romans 5–6
2 Samuel 5–8	Psalm 130	Romans 8

Psalm 27	Ezekiel 11	Romans 10
2 Samuel 22	Psalm 138	1 Corinthians 13
Psalm 30	Ezekiel 36–37	2 Corinthians 1
1 Chronicles 28–29	Psalm 139	2 Corinthians 4
Psalm 31	Daniel 3	2 Corinthians 12
1 Kings 17	Psalm 142	Galatians 5–6
Psalm 32	Daniel 6	Ephesians 3–4
1 Kings 18–19	Psalm 144	Philippians 1
Psalm 33	Joel 2	Philippians 2
2 Kings 4–5:19	Psalm 146	Philippians 3
Psalm 35	Micah 7	Philippians 4
2 Kings 19–20	Psalm 147	Colossians 1–2
Psalm 37	Malachi 3	Colossians 3–4
Nehemiah 1–2	Ezekiel 34	2 Thessalonians 3
Psalm 38	John 10	Hebrews 4
Nehemiah 5–6	Matthew 18	Hebrews 11
Psalm 40	Luke 1	Hebrews 12–13
Job 1–3	John 1	James 1
Psalm 51	Luke 4	James 2–3
Job 42	Luke 5	James 4–5
Psalm 55	Luke 6	1 Peter 1

Proverbs 2–4	Matthew 5	1 Peter 4
Psalm 62	Matthew 6	1 John 1–2
Ecclesiastes 3	Matthew 7	1 John 3–5
Psalm 70	Matthew 8	Revelation 1
Isaiah 6–9	Matthew 9	Revelation 22
Psalm 71	Matthew 10	
Isaiah 25–26	Matthew 11	

Connect with Others in the Gap

One of the biggest things I have learned through my gap travels is that we were not created to do life alone. As people, we are inherently wired for an eternal connection with God in relationship, and we are also designed to connect in community with others to share one another's burdens.

I know firsthand that going through the gap can feel isolating and lonely. It can feel like those around you do not understand your experience or your emotions. One of my greatest prayers through my gap was, "God, please bring people into my life who understand what I am going through." He has been faithful to fill my life with others who were navigating gaps of their own—to encourage me, pray with me, and allow me to do the same for them.

I wanted to create a sacred space where those who are feeling burdened by their gap journeys can come to find support, understanding, and resources for building a safe community for themselves. We have carved out a corner of the online world to do just that, and if you visit www. godofthegaps.org, you will find:

Information on Gap Groups

Gap groups can be started in any community worldwide. These are groups that meet in person at least once a month to talk about faith amid struggle. Leaders will be given monthly resources to share with the group such as video content, podcasts, reading suggestions, discussion questions, and more. Once a group is registered in a community, they will be added to our searchable list so that people going through a gap in your area can find your group and connect with the community being built in your area. Learn how to start or join one in your area.

Soundtracks from the Gap

Music has played a powerful role in my road through the gap. I have created several Spotify® playlists, which you can listen to as you move through your own gap season. I pray these songs bless you, comfort you, strengthen you, and help you to connect deeper to the heart of the God of the gaps.

Recommended Resources

I found wisdom and direction from books, sermons, podcasts, and various tools to help me grow in the gap. I enjoy sharing links to some of my favorites as well as information on new tools to challenge our faith and our personal development through seasons of struggle.

Stories from the Gap

My story is one of the many stories of wrestling with faith through challenging circumstances. I am a strong believer that everyone has a story and every story is important! It was important for me to carve out a space where we could allow people to share their own stories from the gap and how they connected with God on their journeys. I believe stories are powerful teachers, so I invite you to take time to listen and learn from some of the brave and beautiful journeys, shared in this space.

These and other ways to engage can be found online at www.godofthegaps.org. I hope you will connect there and continue the conversation we started in this book. I look forward to hearing your story as well.

About the Author

Christie Love grew up as the quintessential "church kid" who did not fully grasp the difference between religion and a personal relationship with God until she experienced struggles as a young adult. Now she strives to use her lived experience to connect with others who are wrestling with their faith in the face of trials. She has a bachelor's degree in Ministry and Church Leadership and a master's degree in Practical Theology.

In 2011, Christie founded and led an international ministry that challenged women to grow in their faith and leadership. In 2018, she led a team to plant The Connecting Grounds Church in Springfield, MO where she serves as the lead pastor. The church is in an area of the city with profound poverty, with a large number of people living without shelter. In addition to the outreach the church does for the community, Christie is involved in efforts to advocate for social justice, child welfare, economic dignity, and racial healing. She and her husband, Bob, blended families and are blessed by four amazing teenagers.